RISING FEAR

THE SHOOTING SCRIPT

WRITTEN & DIRECTED BY
TOM GETTY

ACROLIGHT
PICTURES
LLC

To family, friends, and supporters of
Rising Fear

Thank you!
- Tom

RISING FEAR

THE SHOOTING SCRIPT
WRITTEN & DIRECTED BY
TOM GETTY

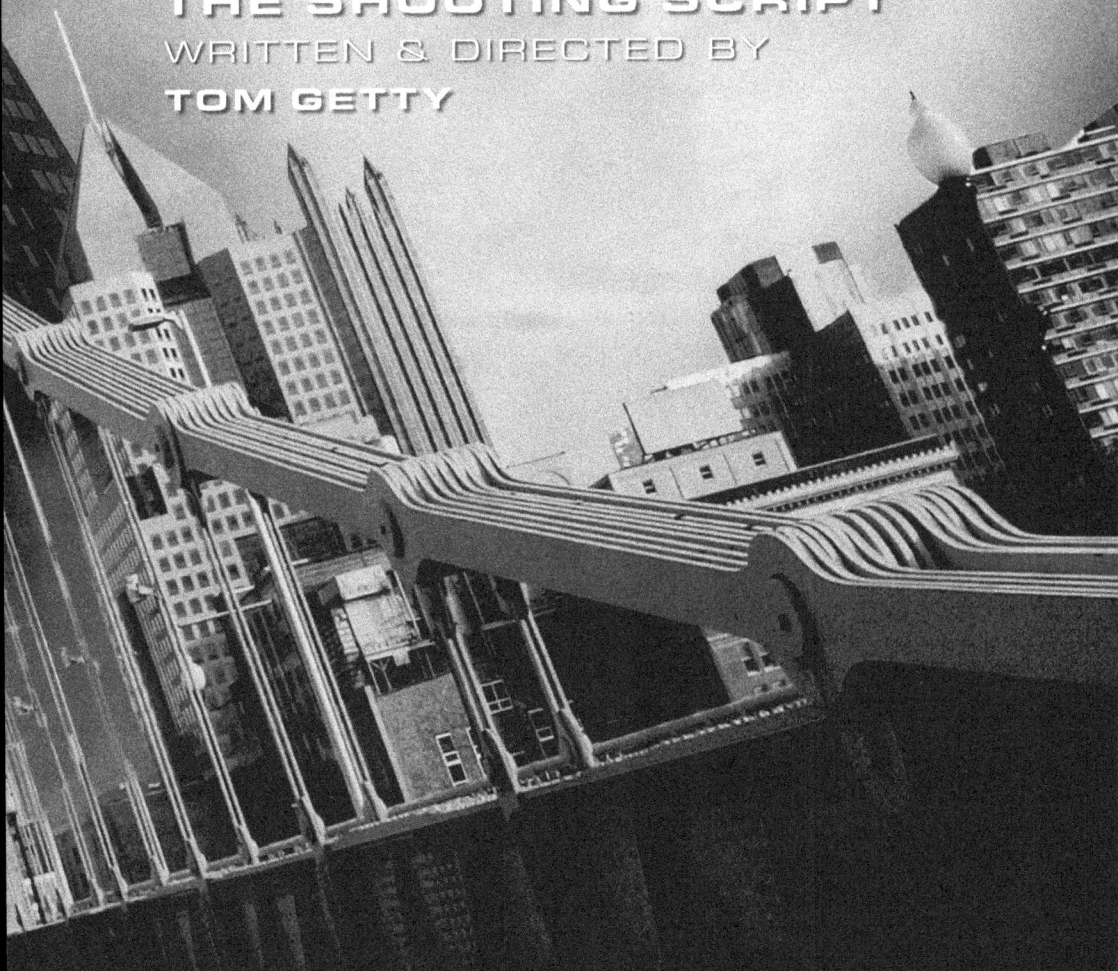

ACROLIGHT
PICTURES
L L C

Storyboard art by Tom Getty.

Photographs by AJ Yaworski
  Matt Meehan
  Chuck Getty
  Tom Getty
  Bill Dill

ISBN: 978-0-9974800-0-9

Designed by Tom Getty

Manufactured in the U.S.A.

1 2 3 4 5 6 7 8 9 10

CONTENTS

PREFACE
FEAR RISES

AN INTERVIEW WITH
TOM GETTY
INTERVIEWED BY CHUCK GETTY

CHUCK: What do they talk about in books like this?

TOM: Writing the story.

CHUCK: The script?

TOM: No, the—story.

CHUCK: You gotta' understand, I'm in the dark about movies. What's the difference between a script and a story?

TOM: The story is the events, the characters. The script is just what people are going to read.

CHUCK: OK. You think we should talk about the story?

TOM: Yes. The story is what's important! Let's talk about the story.

CHUCK: Why did you write this story?

TOM: I wanted to write this kind of movie since I was a boy.

CHUCK: 'Kind' of movie? Like, action?

TOM: Yes. Yes. I wanted to make a *Die Hard*, *Speed* type movie since I was a boy. That was always the major dream. To make—not really to "direct," because you don't know what "directing" is when you're eight—a movie like *Die Hard With A Vengeance*. I begged Mom to take me to see that when it came out—

CHUCK: You saw that when you were in first grade!? Where was I at?

TOM: It was reward for 'acing' a spelling test. That movie is fabulous because it's *Die Hard*, but it's unleashed from the Nakatomi building—that's where the first movie is confined to—and then it sprawls all over New York City. Mom and I are watching that movie—and it just goes. Subway bombs, cab chases, car chases, shooting on the highway, underground—one part he's [Bruce Willis] surfing on a huge truck through "the aqueduct," whatever that is, the fighting, the swearing! No one swears like Bruce Willis!

CHUCK: I don't like foul language.

TOM: I wanted to make a movie like that. How could I make a story like that? And the only place that was similar to New York, that I knew about, was Pittsburgh.

CHUCK: Because of travel hockey.

TOM: How the city [Pittsburgh] looks when you're coming out of the tunnel—it's just THERE—boom. I remember seeing that from when I was a kid. Sitting in the back of the Jeep—isn't it funny we ended up using the same Jeep?—driving on the Parkway, looking up at the buildings. That's where a lot of *Rising Fear* comes from. Sitting in the back of the Jeep, looking out the window at the city, and the Steel building. You were driving me to a game, but I was in the back like Bruce Willis or Keanu Reeves, screeching through traffic, ramming barricades, jumping from one car to the next, jumping off the bypass, rolling onto the ground, commandeering—

CHUCK: Let's not get carried away.

TOM: Right. Anyways. So I'm seeing all of that. Pittsburgh is the greatest!

CHUCK: What did you decide to do with all of that excitement?

TOM: It took years to find something. I didn't want to just, you know—you can't make an entire movie out of acrobatics. But now that I think about it, 9/11 changed the game. For everyone. For movies.

CHUCK: In what way?

TOM: After 9/11, Hollywood stopped making those 90s/80s action movies. No more *Executive Decision*—remember that movie?

CHUCK: With that guy I like. The one from the truck-in-the-desert movie?

TOM: Yea, Kurt Russell in *Breakdown*. No more movies like that. There was one called *Collateral Damage*—fantastic movie—but it was going to open right after 9/11, so they had to bump it.

CHUCK: So, no more movies about terrorists.

TOM: But! They also had a movie in the pipeline called *Sum of All Fears* based on a Tom Clancy novel—that came out in 02' and was a major hit!

CHUCK: So, more movies about terrorists?

TOM: No—they just didn't want to do anymore after that. Which I thought was strange because *Sum of All Fears* was a hit, and *Black Hawk Down*—another war movie—was successful, and I kept thinking, "well, the thinking that no one wants to see a war movie— that's not true." OK, OK—it just came to me.

CHUCK: What?

TOM: I'm organizing my thoughts. After 9/11 is when the superhero movies really took off. And that kind of filled the vacuum for action movies. So instead of John McClane, you had Spider-Man.

CHUCK: That's a shame.

TOM: I like those movies. But they're not, you know. They're not so visceral like *Black Hawk Down*, or *Die Hard*. You don't walk out of a superhero movie thinking, "Gee I hope that never happens. Good thing we have a good American like that John McClane waiting in the wings." The only two superhero movies that actually dealt with the war on terror was *Iron Man* and *The Dark Knight* movies.

CHUCK: This all sounds interesting. But let's get back to *Rising Fear.*

TOM: You mean you don't want to talk about *The Dark Knight?*

CHUCK: I didn't see it, so.

TOM: You didn't see *The Dark Knight?*

CHUCK: That's the one with Jack Nicholson?

TOM: Dad. C'mon.

CHUCK: Yea, yea. Let's get on with this. I have to rake gravel.

TOM: Haha, that's depressing!

CHUCK: Yea, you should make a movie about that!

TOM: *"THE GRAVEL RAKER."* In a trailer voice: "He rakes the gravel." Alright, you're right. I totally lost what we we're talking about. These are all exciting things. I could talk about 90s action movies all day. But we're going to talk about—ah yes. Let's talk about where I felt comfortable about actually writing Rising Fear.

CHUCK: What started you on writing *Rising Fear?*

TOM: I had finished *Emulation*, and I really liked doing that one, and I was still enamored with that idea of the guy being chased by EVERYBODY. I wanted to do another thing like that—like the Hitchcock, guy in the middle of every cross-hair imaginable, *North By Northwest* but with some—

CHUCK: Yea, yea, and?

TOM: I kept trying to come up with some kind of catalyst for a terrorist thriller. I read books. Articles. All kinds of stuff about conspiracies. One idea was a young intern at an investment firm—whatever Bernie Madoff was overseeing. And this intern discovers the Ponzi scheme, and realizes it's going to lead—

CHUCK: Yea, yea, rake gravel, remember?

TOM: I wanted something EXPLOSIVE.

CHUCK: And what lead you to this story?

TOM: I was at the gym, and this girl accidentally left behind her lifting gloves. I gave them to the desk (so I'd have an excuse to talk to her later), and then that night I wondered, "What if she didn't leave those by accident? What if they were meant for someone else? What if someone were watching?"

CHUCK: Who?

TOM: Anyone! FBI, CIA. Terrorists.

CHUCK: Could have been the IRS.

TOM: No! I'm talking—I'm talking BIG!

CHUCK: The IRS is big.

TOM: No—kick-ass big.

CHUCK: You've never been audited. You want to talk about serious ass kickers.

TOM: No but like, this had to be the precursor to something BIG! *Emulation* had this huge plot. Something falls on some little guy, and he unearths this huge conspiracy that will literally end society. I had been listening to that song by the Four Tops, "Wake Me When It's Over." And that—that was the tipping point. That night, this idea about the girl leaving behind her gloves, and dreaming of that song playing over credits of the movie—this is the story.

CHUCK: How long did it take you to write that idea?

TOM: A long time. It took detours.

CHUCK: Surprise.

TOM: It's the process of weeding out bad ideas.

CHUCK: Like?

TOM: I called the script "PANIC" for a while.

CHUCK: Kind of generic?

TOM: I really went through a lot of drafts on that. The story was about a law student then. And it had to do with him stumbling across a terrorist plot—he just moved into his apartment in Pittsburgh, and found evidence that there was going to be a terrorist attack, but then no one believes him, and then he becomes the bad guy, and so he's running through the city. I still like that idea. He would just really kick some serious ass. This law student. You know—I guess subconsciously tailored him after you.

CHUCK: I went to night school. No terrorists.

TOM: But then the terrorist attack was just a front orchestrated by the CIA—or the FBI—or one of them, I can't remember. No, wait. It was the NSA. And the NSA was working with the FBI—and Carter—you know, the part Curtis plays? Yea, he was a SUPER bad guy in this draft. And the whole plot was to create a terrorist attack that would lead to total martial law. Like this is the beginning of *1984*.

CHUCK: Great book.

TOM: Tremendous book. And this would be kind of how that story began. Ok—but anyways. I had the whole thing, like seven drafts down. Spell-checked and everything. And it just.

CHUCK: What happened?

TOM: I met Tom Cruise!

CHUCK: That's a jump.

TOM: Yes. I met him while he was filming *Jack Reacher* in Pittsburgh—and, super nice guy. Amazing. We shook hands and everything. And just that brief encounter made me realize what I actually wanted to do.

CHUCK: Which was?

TOM: I had set the "Panic" story up as a movie that would be sold to a studio, that would have a star, and a 50 million dollar budget. And that didn't work out, and meeting Tom Cruise— and I was watching a lot of Clint Eastwood movies—and I wanted to do something other than just write a story.

CHUCK: Like?

TOM: It's about MAKING a movie.

CHUCK: But movies cost money.

TOM: Millions.

CHUCK: And you had...

TOM: $20 bucks.

CHUCK: So, what?

TOM: I realized, if this story meant so much story me, if this story about fighting terrorism, about THE GUY, the CITY, the BOMB—if it all meant so much to me—you know, and we're going back to when I was a kid sitting in the theater watching *Die Hard III*, and then 9/11, and how you feel about that, and those emotions—and if I really cared, then I would have make the thing myself.

CHUCK: Like 'film' it?

TOM: Yes. And I reached back to that idea about the girl leaving her gloves behind. Something smaller, but still retaining that energy. So the gloves were changed to a cell phone—and then it was shifted around to her asking him to call her, and then the whole thing exploded in my mind, and I started to see how I could take this huge blockbuster movie idea and push it through a no-budget indie film.

CHUCK: Which means?

TOM: I started asking myself how I could actually do it. I realized there would have to be a lot of special effects—the Apache chasing the jeep, the building blowing up, etc.—so I sat down and taught myself Adobe After Effects.

CHUCK: This is a computer program?

TOM: Yes. And Cinema 4d, which deals with 3-D.

CHUCK: Like those blue and red glasses they used to put in cereal boxes?
TOM: No, no. 3-D, as in the dinosaurs from *Jurassic Park*.

CHUCK: I don't follow.

TOM: Like you gotta' make those dinos out of something. Like 3-D. But within the movie. But there were things I needed to learn, and that was one of them. I'm not a special effects guy! But I learned it. And, I knew the movie would need a huge action score, so I contacted Jeff Howanek—he played Kyger in *Emulation*—and asked him where I should start in learning how to do that. I started out playing stuff like "Mary Had A Little Lamb."

CHUCK: A lot to do.

TOM: But it all came out of this energy to tell this story about terrorism—but in a no-budget way. And it would have that look—I'm thinking movies like *The French Connection*, and *To Live and Die In LA*—and you know, I'm looking at movies directors made as their first movie, like Christopher Nolan's *Following*.

CHUCK: Is that the one with the two guys over in…the one where they're in the cafe?

TOM: Britain, I think. But that energy of, "Let's do it!" And those guys did it. Scorsese, Spielberg, Peter Jackson, all of them. They all had to start with that no-budget movie.

CHUCK: Was this yours?

TOM: *Rising Fear.* It would have that gritty, grainy feeling like William Friedkin's *The French Connection.*

CHUCK: With Gene Hackman?

TOM: The grain and all. And we didn't have very good cameras. But that would add to the effect. We came up with all kinds of tricks.

CHUCK: Using me to play the president?

TOM: Yes!

CHUCK: What else?

TOM: Using a teleprompter for the non-actors. So they wouldn't have to memorize lines.

CHUCK: I really liked that.

TOM: Yea, it relaxes people. It's not just reading lines off cue-cards either. Ironically, if you had a pro actor do that, it wouldn't work. But for normal people—boom. Well, anyways. You get your shot. You got the person saying the lines. I just wanted the movie in the can. You know what I mean about that [mimics aiming a camera, grits teeth]?

CHUCK: So *Rising Fear* became a movie you would direct.

TOM: Yes. That summer—2012—I wrote the script the reader is about to read. It was written with all of these thoughts and expectations, and limitations (good limitations), and I had to dig deep. But I'm so proud of the story.

CHUCK: I liked it.

TOM: I felt good about it. I handed it to a few old comrades. Like Anthony Pinto. Christian Condrick. Joce Meehan. She sat down with me and we did a lot of notes. She was the one who suggested getting Kirsten Meenan to play the girl. Even without money, I still believed we could do some of the big budget acrobatics, like with the helicopter, and the building blowing up, and Ground Zero. It got tight—the filming—but we made it. I really think people will enjoy reading this story.

CHUCK: OK, I've gotta' go rake gravel now.

RISING FEAR

THE SHOOTING SCRIPT
DRAFT DATE: 11-11-2012

BY

TOM GETTY

THE ACROLIGHT PICTURES LOGO SWIRLS ON

Blackness. The POWER-ON CHIME of a 2001 DIGITAL VIDEO CAMERA...

The screen fritzes-

...THE LENS OF A VIDEO CAMERA... the red record light turning on...

> MIKEL RAZANOV (V.O.)
> (speaking to camera)
> On September 11th, your nation fell to
> its knees.

The screen fritzes again-

Distant, boxed NEWS FOOTAGE OF:

...A PLANE HITTING THE TRADE TOWERS...

> MIKEL RAZANOV (V.O.)
> You watched as your towers crumbled
> back into the Earth.

PEOPLE SCREAMING...

> MIKEL RAZANOV
> Your citizens groveled through the
> ashes of a once mighty empire...

...of politicians declaring war...

...years passing...2001...2002...2003...the decade from hell...

WAR...

...of soldiers deploying into Afghanistan.

> MIKEL RAZANOV (V.O.)
> You tried standing on your feet.

...fighting... ...the financial collapse of 08'... ...the Nasdaq falling... ...an economy falling to pieces...

All distant, faded news footage. So far away... Time has eaten away at these digital files...

But now they approach closer... and closer...

> MIKEL RAZANOV
> On May the 1st, you found your
> vengeance in claiming a great leader.

...Images of New Yorkers CHANTING, "USA! USA!"

...A newscaster announcing the death of OSAMA BIN LADEN.

> MIKEL RAZANOV
> You chanted and sang songs of joy...
> and peace. You were comforted... by the
> feeling of war's end.

CUT IN:

MIKEL RAZANOV, international terrorist, eyes full of hate, sits in front of the camera, waiting. He is backgrounded by a Taliban flag.

> MIKEL RAZANOV
> But I assure you: Our war is far from
> over.

TITLE: "RISING FEAR"

Mikel Razanov will continue giving this statement/confession throughout the opening scenes....

INT. T-TRAIN - AFTERNOON

Choppy/chaotic guerrilla-style, the confusion of the train passing.

RYAN TAYLOR, aged 26, sits, holding an open book, looking out the window as the train car rushes out of the tunnel's darkness into blinding daylight, the city of Pittsburgh, PA streaming by outside. His eyes adjust, disoriented.

This is a weary ex-soldier, haunted by failure.

He fumbles open a MEDICINE BOTTLE, pops a few pills. Relaxes.

THE T-TRAIN CHUGS ALONG.

INT. WAREHOUSE - CONTINUOUS

Dark. Dreary. A bank of florescent lights FLICKERING ON, only making the chamber more ugly. INTERCUT WITH RAZANOV GIVING HIS STATEMENT...

> MIKEL RAZANOV (V.O.)
> You might have danced in the streets
> when your forces eliminated Usama Bin
> Laden, but today, it is the world who
> will rejoice and stand hand-in-hand as
> Americans grovel through the remains
> of their once proud nation.

SOMEONE placing grungy pesticide jugs down. Placing a funnel inside, pouring in a liquid. This is YAKOV, a Chechen terrorist of Al-Fahad. He looks nervous as he proceeds to construct a BOMB.

INT. T-TRAIN - CONTINUOUS

At a stop. OSKANA ROWAN, pretty, a young professional, early 20s, boards the train. She wears white earbud headphones.

He glances at her from behind his book... and their eyes connect. She hesitates back toward him. He looks down to his pages.

Ryan sees her. Their eyes connect.

She hesitates back toward him. He looks out the window.

> OSKANA
> (gentle)
> May I sit here?

She's indicating to a seat across the aisle from him. The place is virtually empty. He snaps to, trying to be a gentlemen.

> RYAN
> Oh, ha, go ahead.

Despite once being a soldier, his weariness and worldliness only shields a sheepishness, an innocence.

INT. WAREHOUSE - CONTINUOUS

The dreary room again, Yakov continuing to construct the device. Filling the jugs. Screwing them together. Sweat pouring down his forehead, his glasses slipping to the bridge of his nose. Pushing them up.

A few TERRORISTS loom in the back, in the darkness, muttering to one another as they watch...

Yakov inserts a funnel into one of the jugs. Then, with trembling hands, cranes over a teaspoon full of powder...slowly...it's as if merely dropping it could kill them all...

He pours it in.

The terrorists behind try their best to contain their fear.

One of the TERRORISTS motions away from the others, draws his cell phone-

                    TERRORIST
                (into phone)
            It is time...

INT. T-TRAIN - CONTINUOUS

Moving now. The setting sun striking in. Oskana texts on her phone. Ryan watches outside.

                    OSKANA
            So ah... Zack Morris called... he wants
            his cell phone back.

She's indicating to Ryan, sitting there, holding a very old cell phone. He realizes she's talking to him. Sees his shitty phone.

                    RYAN
        Oh, huh?

                    OSKANA
            Hah, you know. "Saved By The Bell,"
            Zack Morris. Your phone.
                (she mimics a big
                  phone from the 90s)
            He wants it back.

Ryan suddenly gets the joke.

                    RYAN
            Oh haha, yea.
                (re: the phone)

Haha, yea. I've been away for a while,
so.

OSKANA
Where's that.

RYAN
Where they don't sell iPhones. I'm
Ryan, by the way. Ryan Taylor.

OSKANA
Yea, I know.

Ryan is taken off guard.

OSKANA
Just kidding. But I've seen you on this
train before.

She smiles...

INT. INDUSTRIAL WAREHOUSE - CONTINUOUS

Yakov continues to construct the bomb... placing down
materials... screwing in screws... drilling holes...

...carefully placing the wires...the reds, the blues, the greens...

INT. T-TRAIN - CONTINUOUS

Ryan and Oskana gab...

RYAN
I've seen you too.

OSKANA
I'm Amanda.

RYAN

I know.

                    OSKANA
Oh do you?

                    RYAN
        (points to her purse)
You had an ID badge clipped to your
purse.

                    OSKANA
What?

                    RYAN
Two weeks ago. I saw you on here...
        (the train...)
With one of those IDs for the TV
station downtown.

Oskana stops at this. Confused.

                    OSKANA
Oh that. I was holding it for my friend.
I'm just interning at the hospital.

                    RYAN
Oh, I see.

                    OSKANA
Today's my last day, though.

                    RYAN
Well congradulations on completing
your internship.

                    OSKANA
Well, today's also my last day riding this

Kirsten Meenan in character.

train...

Ryan glances over at that...

INT. WAREHOUSE - CONTINUOUS

Razanov continues to deliver his confession...

INT. WAREHOUSE - CONTINUOUS

Razanov, continuing to speak to the camera...

> MIKEL RAZANOV
> You see, today is...a lesson...not of
> punishment, but a reminder to all men
> on this earth- that giants do fall, that
> time comes for all towering gods.

Yakov continues building the bomb. Connecting the cell wire.
Tests it. The cell screen lights up, the battery vibrates. He looks
up, nods.

INT. T-TRAIN - CONTINUOUS

Still gabbing.

> OSKANA
> Sooo...I was wondering...what do you
> like to do for fun?

> RYAN
> Uhhmmm... Movies. I like to go to the
> movies.

> OSKANA
> Oh man! Me too!

Oskana broaches another topic...

Rising Fear

-You're great with tension & scenes (visually) in the pacing and how they cut together

- nice intro; specifically "power-on chime" in darkness, then gradually the full image of the video camera, then the voice/image of Razanov

-smooth transition to train scene

- 4 – Oskana seeking him out; motive; good joke

- I like the tension between the interweaving scenes…but it might work better with two separate scenes as opposed to cutting between them. Then again, this might work better once filmed than in the script

- 6 – dialogue feels forced

- 7 – is time passing off screen or is their conversation naturally going from "I watch you"to "what do you do for fun?" ; dialogue unnatural here—strangers—start with coffee or a more casual meet up, even if not going to actually happen; or else a more specific movie that both are excited about

- I'm more interested in the bomb scene at this point than the train scene

- 8 – Good! Internship line. More specific. Character insight. Dialogue stronger on this page. Cut "I'll be waiting…"—too awkward/sinister/misleading. Show their brief relationship develop more. They are two strangers who have seen each other frequently for an extended amount of time.

- Does Ryan look around, smirking? How does he react to this attention—is he used to it? More than just "astonished." Does he look around and make eye contact with another guy, maybe someone else who has been riding the train as frequently as both of them, and acknowledges, possibly in a humorous way, that Ryan got her number?

- Razanov -"dwells" - awk…maybe just "there is"

9 – Has Oskana gotten off at her usual stop? If Ryan has seen her every day, is he curious of her hurried movements? Is this unusual?

Ryan—ex-soldier, and apparent lady's man; initial impression

- Who is Oskana talking to? Unnecessary line?

- Should Razanov's speech finish before train scene? Would help it to be more fluid

Jocelyn Meehan's notes on the script.

>   OSKANA
> What kind?

>   RYAN
> I like em' all.

>   OSKANA
> So, chick flicks.

>   RYAN
> Hhaha, I guess not all.

>   RYAN
> How about you?

>   OSKANA
> Uhm, I'm pretty open minded about
> those things. I love scary movies.

>   RYAN
> Yea, scarys' good!

INT. LOADING BAY - CONTINUOUS

Razanov, talking to the recording camera...

>   MIKEL RAZANOV
> The world will be reminded that David
> can stand against Goliath,

Terrorists load the massive bomb into the back of a utility truck.

EXT. PITTSBURGH STREET - CONTINUOUS

Yakov negotiates the utility van through light traffic. Stopping
for a red light. Waiting patiently.

>   MIKEL RAZANOV (V.O.)

...That even giants can fall at the brave
hands of those willing to pay the price.

Inside, Yakov mutters a prayer.

EXT. SNYDER BUILDING - CONTINUOUS

Yakov pulls the utility van up to the garage entrance and flashes a
BADGE at the SECURITY GUARD.

> SECURITY GUARD
> Can't even keep away on your day off,
> eh?

Yakov nods, drives down into the garage.

INT. SNYDER BUILDING - MAINTENANCE GARAGE
- CONTINUOUS

The UTILITY VAN crawls around a corner, its headlights
igniting, navigating through the mammoth, underground belly of
this skyscraper.

INT. T. TRAIN - CONTINUOUS

He smiles. She smiles, flattered.

INT. SNYDER BUILDING - BASEMENT

Inside the darkness of the utility van...

Yakov squats in the back over the bomb, sweating deeply now.
He flicks a switch- the BOMB HUMS TO LIFE.

He almost awaits for its explosion, but it just sits idle. He takes a
breath, exits the utility van- and SHUTS THE DOOR.

INT. T. TRAIN - CONTINUOUS

Ryan and Oskana, enjoying one another...

THE LOUDSPEAKER ANNOUNCES THAT THEY ARE
APPROACHING "SMITHFIELD" STATION.

> OSKANA
> So, OK. Look. I'll be honest.
> (she broaches the
> subject)
> I don't want to be forward or freak you
> out or anything. But I've seen you on
> this train same time, every day, for the
> past six months... and I just really
> wanted to talk to you.

> RYAN
> Yea?

> OSKANA
> Are you freaked out?

> RYAN
> Haha, no, no, not at all. Not everyday
> you get to talk to a pretty girl!

> OSKANA
> Does your car phone work?
> (indicates toward his
> flip phone)

> RYAN
> That I know of, yes.

She pulls out a piece of paper.

> OSKANA
> Well, my stop is coming up, and I'm

prob not riding this way again.
(she finishes writing)
So...

She hands it over to him. It's her name and number.

OSKANA
I hope it does work.

She gets up to leave...

RYAN
When?

OSKANA
The sooner the better.

She smiles. The train docks.

OSKANA
I'll be waiting.

And she leaves Ryan astonished, holding a number. The train departs.

INT. WAREHOUSE - CONTINUOUS

Razanov... finishing up his confession...

RAZANOV
Today, the world will see... what
cowardice dwells in the American heart.

EXT. STREET - CONTINUOUS

Oskana moves quickly down from the train platform, hurrying away.

RAZANOV (V.O.)

> Your wives, your women, your children
> will all scream for your help, but you
> will find yourself powerless to stop their
> suffering-

INT. T-TRAIN - CONTINUOUS

Ryan sits alone on the train. He smirks, looking at the number.

EXT. STREET - CONTINUOUS

Yakov curbs... and picks up OSKANA.

> RAZANOV (V.O.)
> ...you are all so afraid...

> OSKANA
> I think he bought it.

INT. T-TRAIN - AFTERNOON

Ryan chuckles. Pulls out his phone, DIALS THE NUMBER...

> RAZANOV (V.O.)
> ...But it is not a fear for your country...
> for your freedom... It is only a fear... for
> your own lives.

Ryan hits "SEND."

INT. SNYDER BUILDING - CONTINUOUS

The utility van... sitting alone in the parking garage...

UTILITY VAN

Inside... the bomb sitting quietly...

SUDDENLY THE PHONE'S DISPLAY LIGHTS UP and it

VIBRATES.

Silence.

Then-

DETONATION.

The bomb obliterates the garage in a blinding flash.

EXT. SNYDER BUILDING - CONTINUOUS

The explosion rips through the street, engulfing the building in a roaring ball of fire. Glass shatters. People scream in HORROR.

SNYDER BUILDING - OFFICE FLOORS

Business people going about their day are suddenly VAPORIZED, their hair tangling and blowing as fire appears virtually from nowhere and swallows them whole.

INT. T-TRAIN - CONTINUOUS

Ryan, still holding the cell phone to his ear, listening to the last of the RINGS... as it goes to voice mail.

He rolls his eyes, knowing that "AMANDA" is one of those girls who doesn't pick up her phone.

SNYDER BUILDING

EXPLOSIONS swallow the tower of glass, destroying the sidewalk, eating up the entire structure. Smoke rises. Fire rises.

The city of Pittsburgh lays out before it, silent as the sound of the explosions fade like thunder on a summer evening.

EXT. T-TRAIN STATION - LATER

Ryan exits, strolling down the path, when he notices a gathering of people, all on their cell phones, all looking EXTREMELY concerned.

They all appear to be hypnotized by a bay of HD TVs playing the NEWS.

Ryan approaches, looking at the TV screen. A NEWSCASTER REPORTS...

> NEWSCASTER (V.O.)
> 5:12 PM eastern time, in downtown
> Pittsburgh, a large explosion has just
> occurred at Forbes and 2nd at, I believe,
> the Snyder building.

Ryan is captured by the horror on television, by the image of the SNYDER building in downtown Pittsburgh already engulfed in flames.

> NEWSCASTER (V.O.)
> Right now you are looking at a live feed
> of what appears to be the Snyder
> building. You can see the smoke
> billowing out.

Ryan glances around at the other people gawking at the screens, on their phones talking to family and loved ones, trying to hold back tears, puffy red eyes.

> PERSON
> (to phone)
> Are we being attacked?

A mother squeezes her child's hand.

On television, they continue elaborating on the horror in downtown Pittsburgh. Ryan just watches...

Two children watch... not quite knowing what to make of it.

Another September 11th, unfolding before their very eyes.

INT. RYAN'S APARTMENT - LATER

Ryan enters, turns on the TV, which continues to expound on the horror in downtown Pittsburgh...

                    NEWSCASTER
          ...We are in fact getting word that, yes,
          this is a terrorist attack.

-- NOTE -- SEE APPENDIX FOR EXPANDED NEWS COVERAGE -- The newscasters talk about the fire fighters heroically risking their lives to save the people inside, heading off toward their doom.

Ryan shakes his head, saddened. He sits down. Sighing.

The news continues. Ryan consider the number Oskana gave him (again, he thinks her name is "AMANDA"). He can't believe he's doing it again, but-

Dials in her number.

EXT. NATIONAL SECURITY AGENCY - SAME

The massive intelligence building sprawls below...

INT. N.S.A. - HALLWAY - SAME

An NSA TECH, young, hurries through a hall, loosening his tie, clutching a cell phone, clutching a laptop.

                    NSA TECH
          Put me through to Bannings. Yes, to
          Bannings. We just got lucky: our guy

must have found out one of his bombs'
didn't go off.

He rushes into a

TECH ROOM

Awash in screens and empty computers. He slams the laptop
down. Fires up the screen, typing rapidly.

> NSA TECH
> Because he keeps trying to call it! I'm
> running a trace right now.

INT. RYAN'S APARTMENT - SAME

Ryan waits on the RINGING PHONE. Considering the
number. Gets fed up. Crumbles the number, tosses it.

> RYAN
> (to himself)
> What a schmuck.

INT. TECH ROOM - SAME

The NSA tech peers into his computer screen in disbelief.

> NSA TECH
> Suspect just got off the line, but the
> signals' still registering strong.

Furiously strikes the keyboard.

ON SCREEN - A SATELLITE MAP rushes through
AERIAL PHOTOGRAPHS WITH SPEED, ZEROING IN
ON PITTSBURGH...

> NSA TECH

Pittsburgh...

THE SATELLITE CONTINUES ZEROING IN...

> NSA TECH
> Mt. Lebanon- coordinates, alpha, delta,
> six, niner-

Then- BEEP.

> NSA TECH
> Bingo!

The aerial photographs ZERO IN ON AN APARTMENT,
HIGHLIGHTS THE CELL SIGNAL and a box flashes up
identifying:

> NSA TECH
> Ryan H. Taylor, address three-one-nine
> north diamond, Pittsburgh, PA, zip
> code one-five-two-zero-one!

> NSA TECH
> Houston, I believe you have your man.

EXT. NEIGHBORHOOD - LATER

A black SUBURBAN screeches up. FEDERAL AGENTS
RON CARTER and MIKE ARLEN exit, appraising the scene.
Carter holds a radio to his ear, listening to CHATTER.

> ARLEN
> (to Carter)
> NSA and our offices just confirmed: the
> cell phone and apartment are both
> registered to the guy on the lease. We
> have triple confirmation.

I loved the look of this location. It had a William
Friedkin, *Exorcist* feel to it.

> RADIO (V.O.)
> ...all units positioned at elm and smith.
> Units B and C will proceed in tag
> formation.

> CARTER (V.O.)
> Whatever happens, we take this guy
> alive.

Carter signals to a group of SWATS, "READY IT UP!"

SWATS hunker down in formation, locking and loading their assault rifles. Their radios CRACKLE LIGHTLY.

INT. RYAN'S APARTMENT - BATHROOM - SAME

He showers, oblivious.

In the other room, the TV continues to play a news broadcast of the PRESIDENT OF THE UNITED STATES giving a speech...

> PRESIDENT
> ...Tomorrow, I will be traveling to
> Pittsburgh, Pennsylvania to visit with
> the emergency personnel and rescue
> workers at Ground Zero...

And Ryan's phone...sitting there.

EXT. RYAN'S APARTMENT - SAME

FBI agents, SWAT teams, both getting ready for war. Strafing between the low-rent houses, kicking through gates, their radios humming quietly.

INTERCUT:

- RYAN GETTING OUT OF THE SHOWER, DRYING HIS HAIR, GETTING DRESSED...

- The SWATS strafing.

- The FBI agents, moving in.

> CARTER
> (to Arlen)
> Make sure the engines' running...

RYAN'S APARTMENT

Ryan combs his hair, continues eyeing the television as the president finishes his ultimatum to all terrorists everywhere...

> PRESIDENT
> Today... we are faced with a rising
> fear... but in face of that fear... we will
> not buckle... we will not waiver... and
> we will not fall to our knees.

OUTSIDE HIS APARTMENT

SWATs have finished strafing.

> SWAT #1
> Green light...

RYAN'S APARTMENT

A moment of silence... and just as the secretary finishes his speech—

BAM! The SWATS explode in, Ryan reacts with total surprise and panic! He instinctively retracts into one of the other rooms, taken completely off guard.

The SWATS roar and rampage through, letting their assault rifles and flashlights attached to the barrels lead the way, their goggles and masks just making them indifferent monoliths.

They tackle Ryan, cuff him immediately. Ryan protests and screams, wanting to know what in the hell is going on.

ONE SWAT MEMBER CRACKS HIM OVER THE HEAD WITH HIS RIFLE...

Ryan immediately stops.

OUTSIDE

Two SWATS drag a limp and fading Ryan out, down the sidewalk. Fast.

On the street, a suburban SCREAMS up. The door is opened, and the SWATs throw Ryan in there. Shutting the door, sealing him in.

Immediately the truck screeches off into the fading light...

INT. INDUSTRIAL BUILDING - STORAGE FACILITY - HALLWAY - NIGHT

The SWATs drag Ryan through double doors, through hallways laden with grease and dirt. Florescent lights hum above, casting an ugly garish gloom over his face and his captors.

He's barely coming to, trying to figure out what's going, trying to step up right. But he keeps fading.

INT. STORAGE FACILITY - ROOM - NIGHT

Ryan, bound to a chair by plastic cuffs. Still out of it. He slowly awakens, slowly becoming aware of the gloomy surroundings, of his bindings.

Carter emerges from the darkness carrying a chair, sits it down in front of Ryan.

> RYAN
>
> Look, I don't know...I don't know who you think I am, but... you got the wrong guy.

> CARTER
>
> Oh- well-

Carter flips the chair around, sits backward on it, getting comfy. He places a folder on the table, opens it to reveal a DOSSIER ON RYAN.

> CARTER
>
> This is you right? Ryan Taylor... trained at Quantico, special operations command, MARSOC leader.

Ryan... looking at him... not quite sure what's going on... why he's here... or why he's cuffed to a chair by those zip cuffs you see cops use on drunks.

> RYAN
>
> What is going on?

> CARTER
>
> This is you, yes?

> RYAN
>
> Yes...

> CARTER
>
> Then all I need is a signature...

Carter presents the cuffed Ryan with a thicket of paper. Ryan

TRAL INTELLIGENCE BULLETIN

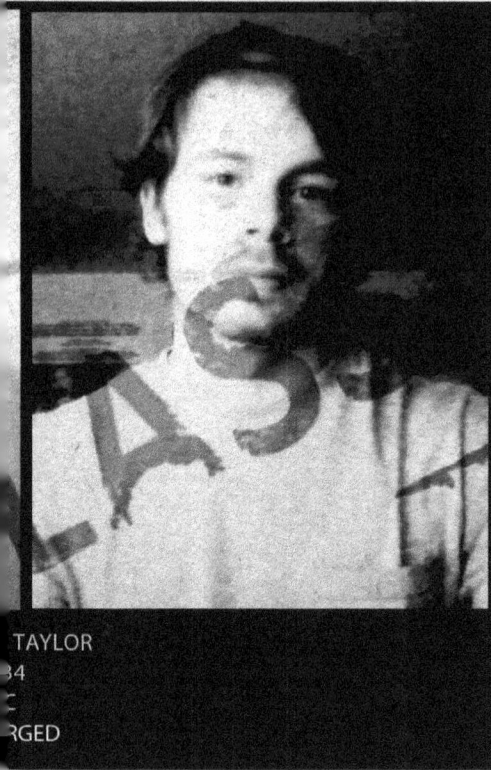

RYAN T. TAYLOR

DATE OF BIRTH:	08/14/1987
CITZEN:	AMERICAN
WEIGHT:	165 LBS
MARTIAL STATUS:	SINGLE
CHILDREN:	NONE
LANGUAGE:	ENGLISH
MILITARY SERVICE:	USMC, MARSOC
MARKS:	SCAR ON UPPER LIP
HAIR COLOR:	RED
EYE COLOR:	GREEN
CURRENT RESIDENCE:	PITTSBURGH, PA

TAYLOR
34

RGED

n Taylor, leader of Marsoc unit, was reported AWOL on December 16,2008. He had
a stationed at Camp Eggers in Kabul, Afghanistan. It is reported that he followed a clas-
d tip of the location of a terrorist training camp n

nfiltrated the camp   as a member of Al Qadea. While inserted, he befriended
                         His main objective
ma Bin Laden. However, his objective
ide bombing at US Embassy.   fled to nearest CIA base.

n Taylor has been flagged as a threat to national security. His allegiance is of high suspi-
                                                             vital intel on high value
rist targets, and sleeper cells. He is to be placed under watch, and considered danger-

peers at it.

CARTER
The important material is on the front.

Ryan sees words about waiving his rights... about confessing...

RYAN
What the hell is this!?

CARTER
It's an agreement-
(pause)
To not bring your case to trial.

RYAN
What trial...?

Ryan sees the video camera filming all of this...

CARTER
In exchange we will see that your
sentence is significantly reduced and
that you serve your sentence in a state
psychiatric facility-

RYAN
I'm sorry, who are you?

CARTER
I'm Ron Carter... federal agent with the
FBI.

Flashes Ryan his badge... then tosses it over on a table, out of the
way- a gesture that says, "get comfy..."

CARTER
I'm currently investigating the Snyder

building bombing...and right now,
you're my prime suspect.

Pushing in on Ryan... as his face cascades in horror...

                    RYAN
        No... you... you got the wrong guy.
        Wait, a second... wait... you got the
        wrong guy...

Carter holds up Ryan's cell phone, now zipped up in a plastic
baggie. EVIDENCE.

                    CARTER
        This is your cell phone, right?

                    RYAN
        No!

                    CARTER
        We have you not once... but three times
        calling the bomb. The SIM card and
        the phone company's records confirm
        it. Not to mention yours are the only
        prints on the cell.

                    RYAN
        No... my god...

Ryan...realizing in horror... in terror...

                    CARTER
        Ryan... you killed 76 people.

Ryan tries denying it... even to himself...

                    RYAN
        No... no... my god... no.

CARTER
Ryan... you killed 76 people...

RYAN
A girl gave me the number.

CARTER
This is someone your working with?

RYAN
What? No. This girl I met on the T-
train- she gave me her number to call-
yes- I called it- but... my god- I didn't-

Carter, not wanting to listen to this bullshit-

CARTER
Look, all I need from you is a signature.

RYAN
Her name's Amanda. She works at
KDTA- I saw her badge- she's about
5'9-

Carter, in a flash, grabs Ryan's collar, twisting it, rage flashing
across his face.

CARTER
If it were up to me I'd hand you over to
the American people so they could
lynch your ass at Ground Zero. God
knows they need it. But I'm just a
messenger.

Carter drops a pen for Ryan to sign it.

CARTER

And your friends want this agreement
signed. Six hours ago.

                    RYAN
Who?

                    CARTER
The CIA...

Ryan, realizing something with deep terror-

                    RYAN
It's a set up! Carter! You've got the
wrong guy! I'm being set up! I didn't
know!

But Carter slams the door on him, cutting off his voice.

INT. OTHER ROOM - SAME

Carter drops the tough guy act a little bit. Arlen approaches him.

                    ARLEN
What's the CIA want with him?

                    CARTER
That's between him and them. I'm just
a messenger.

                    ARLEN
What about the girl he mentioned?
The one from KDTA.

Carter glances over at the Tech on the phone-

                    TECH
            (pressing the phone
            against his shoulder)

31

Night manager says there's no Amanda
in the whole building.

Carter accepts that.

INT. INTERROGATION ROOM - LATER

Ryan sits there... looking at the confession sheet... almost
despondent... but clearly wracked with guilt inside... with fear...
with remorse.

He glances up at the news playing on the television... playing the
images of the carnage...

Ryan can hardly contain his pain.

INT. CORRIDOR - LATER

Carter stands amidst the shadows, huddled on a cell phone,
talking in whispers...

> CARTER
> No, we he hasn't signed yet.

> BANNINGS (V.O.)
> Well, we're going on 5 AM.

> CARTER
> I told you- he keeps telling us to find
> this girl.

> BANNINGS (V.O.)
> It's a bullshit evasion tactic. The guys'
> trained for that.

> CARTER
> What do you want me to do?

Mikel

Slightly more character build up with Ryan.
Nonverbal — A detailed look at his apt that
gives clues as to his past + personality.

President could be in car during the carjacking
to bring upon some humor

To get rid of the Attack Chopper
Ryan could swerve into a car garage
to get ~~into cover~~ and also get above
the Chopper and use the rocket launcher.

Some timing issues with the ~~bomb~~ surface and the
reactions of the people after hearing the
CIA was the cause.

Are these news updates being pushed through the
iPad display — that could be a less obtrusive way
to get those broadcasts into the scene and also
further Mikel's sinister actions to poke and
taunt and slowly reveal his creation.

A guest that could have already been on the news
program could be the one who antagonizes this issue
and in turn creates the movement that brings upon

Curtis Caldwell's notes on the script.

> BANNINGS
> At this point. Whatever. They want
> assurance that we can just put him
> away.

> CARTER
> I don't understand. Why is the CIA
> want this so bad?

> BANNINGS (V.O.)
> Above your paygrade, son.

> CARTER
> But don't you think it's odd? Some
> asshole blows up a building in
> downtown Pittsburgh and the CIA is
> willing to protect him?

INT. RAZANOV'S HIDEOUT - BEDROOM - EARLY MORNING

Gauzy, early morning light. Still dark almost. Razanov rises
from his mattress on the floor. He kneels.

YAKOV appears at the doorway.

> YAKOV
> Mikel... the networks are showing it.

> RAZANOV
> Then it has begun.

INT. STORAGE FACILITY - SAME

Carter, still on the phone with Bannings.

> BANNINGS (V.O.)
> I don't think it's him so much as

themselves they're trying to protect.

                    CARTER
From what?

                    BANNINGS (V.O.)
The media. Get that signature.

Bannings hangs up. Carter stands there, pondering that. His
radio crackles-

                    CARTER
Go ahead.

                    TECH (V.O.)
You need to see this.

Carter moves down the corridors, enters-

THE SECURITY ROOM

Where the TELEVISION BLARES. On screen, supered by
the CXN logo, a MASKED TERRORIST (Razanov concealing
his identity) SPEAKS.

INTERROGATION ROOM

Ryan sees this on TV as well...

SECURITY ROOM

Everyone watches as the masked terrorist spews his hatred....

                    TECH
            (to Carter)
        CXN just got this 15 minutes ago via e-
        mail.

Carter watches-

MASKED TERRORIST
...Yesterday was but a prelude to the
misery coming for your people. You
haven't even begun to understand the
suffering that is in store for your
pathetic nation.

CARTER
(to Tech)
Run a search on where the videos'
coming from...

The tech rushes to the keyboard.

TECH
The e-mail's IP address is coming out
of...Madrid- no- Khost, Bangalor...
Tokyo!

ARLEN
It's a mirrored server.

MASKED TERRORIST
...you who have invaded our
countries...you who have dared step
forth on our sacred land...you who dare
try and shake our cause by murdering
our leader USAMA BIN
LADEN...know this: your time has
come. Come nightfall, your land will
once again be drenched in blackness
and strewn in ruins. The world will
rejoice as judgment is finally served
upon the west. You might think you
have apprehended one of my soldiers...

but I assure you, you have nothing.

RYAN

Watches with fear, realizing with dread that they're turning the light on him.

CARTER

Looking in on Ryan. His phone rings, he answers it.

> BANNGINGS (V.O.)
> Are you seeing this?

> MASKED TERRORIST
> ...now...I won't tell you when and
> where...but know...that your country, by
> the end of the day, will be on its knees.

> BANNINGS (V.O.)
> Carter, you've got authorization from
> justice. Find the next attack.

The masked terrorist vanishes from the screen, leaving aghast newscasters, trying to fumble along.

Carter hangs up, looks out at Ryan, who knows he's now in deep shit.

Carter charges in.

> CARTER
> Where is it!?

> RYAN
> I don't know who that guy is, or what
> he was saying-

Carter flips the table over and lunges at Ryan-

CARTER
Where is the next attack!?

Ryan doesn't know how to answer... looking in the man's eyes...

RYAN
I dont know.

Carter looks in Ryan's eyes... then:

CARTER
(to tech)
Turn off the camera.

Fear washes over Ryan as the tech rushes to the camera, shuts it
off, caps the lens.

RYAN
What are you doing? What are you
doing?!

Carter just walks away, trying to contain his rage.

RYAN
Please- look, I'm telling you, you're
making a huge-

One of the agents DOUSES HIM WITH A BUCKET OF
WATER. Ryan, stunned. He tries clearing the water out of his
eyes, his hands still bound.

Then, an agent wheels an UNGAINLY LOOKING
MACHINE IN. It's equipped with dials, gauges, and knobs...
and jumper cables.

Ryan looks up, sloshing the water out of his eyes. He sees them plugging it in.

> RYAN
> What are you doing? What are you
> doing?

Carter holds up Ryan's AGREEMENT SHEET WITH THE CIA.

> CARTER
> On behalf of the American people, the
> CIA can eat their deal.

Rips it up.

The machine FIRES to life, the gauges JUMPING. Ryan realizes with horror: They're going to give him shock torture.

> RYAN
> NO! NO! NO!

Carter strikes the jumper cables together, sparks igniting. The other agents just watch disappointedly.

> RYAN
> You got the wrong guy! I'm telling you!
> Please, please, let me call someone, let
> me call someone!

But Carter just jams the one jumper cable into Ryan's gut, holding it there as the ex-soldier convulses. The lights flicker.

Carter removes the jumper cable. Ryan recovers, his eyes completely stunned.

> CARTER
> Now. You're going to tell us... where is
> will the next strike be?

RYAN
Jesus Christ... I'm an American.

Carter ZAPS HIM AGAIN. Then stops.

CARTER
Denver, New York, LA, Seattle,
Miami- you tell us and this all goes
away.

Ryan... growing delirious...

RYAN
You have NO idea what you're getting
into!

CARTER ZAPS HIM AGAIN! THIS TIME HOLDS IT
IN.

CARTER
GIVE ME A LOCATION!

He yanks back. Ryan tries gathering himself. Carter waits.
Ryan...

RYAN
Please... I...

The agent DOUSES RYAN AGAIN, the water cascading over
his head, down ACROSS HIS WRIST TIES.

Carter strikes the jumper cable again-

RYAN
No! No! Wait! No!

Carter stops. Ryan, a shamble of a man... broken.

                    RYAN
        LA...

Everyone listens...

                    RYAN
        The location of the next attack is LA.

Carter, kneeling...

                    CARTER
            Where?

                    RYAN
        Downtown. The collesuem.

Carter retracts, motions to his other agent.

                    CARTER
        Find out who the guy in the mask is...

Carter walks away, dropping the JUMPER CABLES near the
very large puddle of water that divides the room...

Carter gets on his cell, far away, to check the information. Ryan
sees this...

And behind him... his bindings are still wet...and he wriggles
them around.

                    AGENT
        So what are ya' doin' it for? Allah?
        They paying you?
            (saying Osama)

Ryan continues to wriggle his bindings.

                    AGENT

You in bed with Ew-Sama? Huh... you
fucking traitor.

Ryan's eyes roll in the back of his head, he begins to GAG.

The agent alerts.

> AGENT
> Hey- cut that shit.

Ryan goes into full on- convulsions.

> AGENT
> Carter!

Carter is on the phone.

> CARTER
> Get a handle on him!

Ryan shudders deeply, his eyes turning white. The agent shakes
his head in disgust, moves over to crack Ryan on the head-

But Ryan suddenly rips his hands through the wetted bindings,
spinning the agent around, unholstering the agent's 9MM
Beretta, and jamming the pistol at the agent's head.

Everyone reacts, pulling their guns on him. He uses the agent as
a shield-

> RYAN
> Stop! Stop! I'll pull the trigger!

Carter re-enters, drawing his weapon.

> RYAN
> Just...everyone...stop.

Carter and the other agents keep their weapons on him.

> AGENT
>
> Ryan, you don't wanna'-

> RYAN
>
> Shut up! Look. You.
> (to Carter)
> You and me are both being set up.

> CARTER
>
> Then let's put our guns down and talk
> about it?

Ryan looks at him, "c'mon."

> CARTER
>
> There's five of us and one of you Ryan-
> and even with your training-

Ryan kicks the jumper cables still on the ground in the puddle of water- SPARKS FLY IN THE AIR, BLINDING THE AGENTS. Ryan cracks his hostage over the head, dashes out of there, shutting and locking the door behind him.

HALLWAY

He checks and loads the 9MM as he escapes down the corridor.

INTERROGATION ROOM

Carter is able to kick away the jumper cables.

> CARTER
>
> Lock down the exits!

HALLWAY

Ryan hears the door opening behind him, agents emerging, FIRING. He ducks out of the way. Fires back- but does so to intentionally miss them.

The agents fire back.

He escapes out a back door, breaking it open, emerging out into the

EARLY MORNING

Dawn light. Confused as to where he is. He races off.

HALLWAY

The agents emerge, racing out the door. They look around outside, can't find Ryan. Carter directs them in different directions and they sprawl out to find him.

RYAN

He races down the street, wiping water from his face, fixing himself, looking back.

CARTER

Moving along with his other agents. Breaking off, seeing the wet foot prints.

RYAN

Moving along. Suddenly- BANG! BANG! Out of the darkness. He ducks away. Carter and his men appear, chasing. Ryan runs.

He leads them down a maze of alleyways and tight spaces, running, racing. They keep firing. He fires back, again, not trying to hit them.

CARTER

Breaks off from his men, going down a corridor on his own.

Moving around, looking for Ryan-

When all of a sudden- CLICK! Ryan emerges from the darkness, gun at Carter's face. He's got the drop on him. Carter knows he's fucked.

> CARTER
> Just tell me. Where is the next attack
> going to be...

> RYAN
> We'll find out , won't we?

Ryan knocks something down that traps Carter for a second while Ryan runs.

RYAN

Breaking away toward the horizon now, moving down a street, the sun striking up. He moves into an alleyway, climbs up a building.

He emerges up top a one story building, looking over across the river at the city of Pittsburgh.

CARTER

Emerges onto the same street, triggering his radio that Ryan made it onto this street. He's searching around in the morning light, looking behind cars.

Little does he know that he's right above him on the building.

RYAN

...moving along on the rooftops...

But then suddenly, he's out of space.

AGENTS

Racing onto the street, one of them radioing that they're shutting down the block.

Suburbans screech onto the street.

Ryan has no where to go.

CARTER

Looking around. He approaches the INCLINED PLANE front office, looking at the inclined plane, people getting on.

He flashes his badge at the operator, enters the car, looks around for Ryan. Finds nothing. Grits in frustration.

RYAN

Up above still, looking around. Worried. He can hear the agents running around below. The dogs BARKING.

Then- he hears the DEPARTURE BELL RING!

CARTER - STREET LEVEL

Still looking around. But what he doesn't see: behind him, the inclined plane departing, descending the tracks- and Ryan jumping ONTOP OF THE CAR... and riding out of site.

And there he goes: Ryan, riding the inclined plane... kneeling on top of the car, holding on, steadying his fears...

Sitting on top of the car, riding down, he pulls out something and looks at it:

IT'S AGENT CARTER'S BADGE...

...and the city of Pittsburgh approaching far in the background, the sun striking Ryan's face.

...and Carter, defeated.

INT. MARINE ONE HELICOPTER - MORNING

Looking through a dirty window at the city of Pittsburgh... smoke still pouring from the Snyder building.

The president, now dressed in civilian garb, contemplates through the window.

A concerned AIDE sits beside him, hushed voiced:

> AIDE
> Mr. President, I just received a report
> that the primary suspect of the Snyder
> bombing just escaped custody.

The president doesn't answer.

> AIDE
> And... the Secret Service feels its
> pertinent that your return to
> Washington. They're preparing a
> secure bunker.

The president keeps looking out the window at the burning city.

> PRESIDENT
> Ken, when you look down there...
> (re: the city)
> What do you see?

> AIDE
> I see a city.

PRESIDENT

...I see a country...under siege.
(deeper)
I see good people...held hostage by a
man cowering in a cave.
(to Ken)
I made a promise to the American
public that I would keep them safe.
And I can't do that hiding in an
underground bunker.

AIDE

Mr. President, the Secret Service is
already anxious enough taking you
through Ground Zero. They have no
idea what the situation's like down
there. And now that one of the
terrorists is free... the risks are just too
great.

PRESIDENT

Evil has found its way to our shoreline
and it threatens to destroy everything-
our freedoms, our liberties... our lives.
We are faced with a rising fear... and
cannot turn our backs to it.
(beat)
Not anymore.

The Aide, after a minute...

AIDE

I'll inform the White House.

EXT. PITTSBURGH - GROUND ZERO - MORNING

News coverage of fire fighters and FEMA workers helping at ground zero, cleaning up, sifting through the rubble. Dreary. Miserable.

EXT. PITTSBURGH - GOLDEN TRIANGLE - SAME

Ryan emerges his away from an alleyway, keeping his head down...

Pushes his way through morning foot traffic... entering a park of corporate towers.

He passes a marble stone sign that says "KDTA TV 5." Enters the tall building.

INT. KDTA TV 5 - MAIN LOBBY - SECONDS LATER

Ryan approaches the DESK SECURITY GUARD, flashes his badge-

> RYAN
> Special Agent Carter, can I speak with
> your human resources director?

EXT. PARK - MT. WASHINGTON - MORNING

Carter lays a map of Pittsburgh down over the hood of his Suburban, using a grease pencil to mark a perimeter.

> CARTER
> 15 miles out- 579, 376, all west and
> eastbounds- close em' down.

> ARLEN
> Toward the airport...

> CARTER
> (shaking his head

"no")
Midtown.

He marks the grease pencil-

CARTER

Start there and work your way out.

Carter looks over the map... in toward the middle of the city.

INT. KDTA TV - HUMAN RESOURCES DEPARTMENT - SAME

HR REP leads Ryan through a corridor to a row of computers.

HR REP

Do you think someone here might have been involved?

RYAN

No, no. We just want to run a brief check on everyone. Cover all our bases.

HR REP

OK. Well- all departments of personal are listed here. Times they worked here, files.

She LOGS HIM INTO A COMPUTER TERMINAL. He takes a seat.

RYAN

Just what I need.

HR REP

You look so familiar.

He smiles at her.

                         RYAN
            I get that all the time.

EXT. PARK - MT. WASHINGTON - SAME

                         TECH
            Why would he risk going into the city?

                         CARTER
            Because the plans not finished.

He marks the words "GROUND ZERO" where the Snyder
building is located.

                         ARLEN
            You think the next attack is going to be
            here?

                         CARTER
            I didn't say that.

                         TECH
            Ahh c'mon, the whole city is locked
            down. You got FEMA workers, the
            national guard, and every cop in a 20
            mile radius.

Carter sees a news reporter talking on one of the laptops...

                         CARTER
            Then I think Mr. Taylor's deal with the
            CIA is about to expire...

INT. KDTA TV - HR DEPARTMENT - SAME

Ryan's fingers striking the keyboards, clicking through the files
and records of everyone who works at KDTA. Cameramen,
reporters, janitors, security guards, anchorwomen...

Picture after picture.

THE TV PLAYS NEWS HOW THE PRESIDENT IS
ARRIVING AT PITTSBURGH INTERNATIONAL.

LATER

Ryan still continues to strike through the pictures-

Then, one catches his eye. It's the girl, OSKANA. He stares
into the eyes of her picture. It raises the hairs on the back of his
neck. He sees her name is OSKANA ROWAN. It lists her as a
cameraman. Her status is that of an intern. She studies at RMU
and plays soccer in her free time.

He sees the word "DEPARTMENT: NEWS." He picks up the
phone, hits the button for the news department. It RINGS. A
WOMAN ANSWERS.

> WOMAN (V.O.)
> Yes?

> RYAN
> Hi, yes, I'm trying to get in touch with
> an Oskana Rowan up there in the news
> department...

> WOMAN (V.O.)
> I'll see if she's here.

Then, on TELEVISION, NEWS BREAKS. It immediately
catches Ryan's eye-

> REPORTER
> The alleged trigger man of the Snyder
> building bombing and sole suspect of
> yesterday's deadly terrorist attack has

escaped federal custody in a dring chase
through the Mt. Washington district...

His face drops, the reporter explaining what happened, and
then... SHOWING HIS PICTURE.

                    REPORTER
          This is the man federal authorities are
          saying is armed and dangerous.

The WOMAN COMES BACK ON THE LINE.

                    WOMAN (V.O.)
          I'm sorry, I can't find her.

                    RYAN
          That's fine. Do you know where she
          might be?

                    WOMAN
          Well, she called in sick... try her cell.

                    RYAN
          Thank you.

Hangs up. Ryan looks at the computer, sees her address...

Prints out the file on her. On TV they continue to bad mouth
him.

UPSTAIRS

The HR REP, chatting with her friend, notices the news
report...realizes that the SAME GUY IS DOWNSTAIRS. Slips
off quietly.

EXT. PITTSBURGH - 376 - SAME

Carter and team roll along in their suburban. Carter listens to
BANNINGS on the cell phone...

> BANNINGS (V.O.)
> What the hell do you think you're
> doing!?

> CARTER
> It was the only way I could get a lead
> on him.

> BANNINGS (V.O.)
> Do you know what these guys at the
> CIA are capable of?

> CARTER
> Not giving us information.

> BANNINGS (V.O.)
> No, we didn't give you information.
> And if this gets any larger, it's you
> whose going to answer to the shit
> storm.

> CARTER
> From where? Langley?

> BANNINGS
> Washington has many corridors of
> power, Carter.

> CARTER
> Bannings, who is this guy?

> BANNINGS (V.O.)
> You find him before the president gets
> there. That's all.

Banngings HANGS up. The tech's computer BEEPS-

> TECH
> OK- Gateway Plaza. 441.

He flicks on the sirens.

> ARLEN
> What's there?

> CARTER
> Who do you think?

HR DEPARTMENT

Ryan looks over the address, his eyes scanning.

He goes back to the computer, calls up GOOGLE. He types in the address... and then adds the word "REALITY."

A list of REALITY websites pop up- but the first search is a website for a realty company that leases the girl's apartment.

STANWIX STREET

The Suburban screeches down the street, sirens wailing.

HR DEPARTMENT - SAME

Ryan clicks on the website's link...

"AMERICANA REALTY" crops up- a phone number... and address. He writes that down.

STAIRWELL

The girl moves down the steps.

HR DEPARTMENT

Ryan rips the piece of paper off, leaves. The news continues to caution people about him.

EXT. KDTA TV - MOMENTS LATER

Ryan, folding up the paper, pocketing his hands, disappears into an alleyway.

INT. RAZANOV'S HIDEOUT - SAME

The news playing, people lambasting Ryan, how he betrayed his country. Razanov turns to Oskana...

> RAZANOV
> It seems like things are going smoothly.

EXT. KDTA - GATEWAY PLAZA - SAME

The Suburban SUV screeches up. Carter and team roll out, heading for the building.

INT. KDTA - HR DEPARTMENT - SAME

The HR REP leads them back to where Ryan was...

> HR REP
> Security shut down the whole building
> as soon as we saw the news, so I can't
> imagine he got out.

Carter knows better though...

> CARTER
> What did he want down here?

> HR REP
> Uhmm, he said something about
> wanting to look through personnel files.

She shows him the computer station. The screen is off... He looks on the desk and something catches his eye:

His badge. He picks it up, not saying anything. Touche. He nods.

Then he sees that the badge was holding down a piece of paper-the girl's personal file. Her picture. Her name. Carter picks it up, looks it over, looks at the girl, looks at all the information.

The tech, still clicking away at his laptop, emerges-

>   TECH (O.S.)
>   It's here!

Carter glances over.

>   TECH
>   The server the video came from. It
>   came from an apartment here, in
>   Pittsburgh.

Carter glances back down at the girl's address..."BEECHWOOD BLVD."

>   CARTER
>   In Squirrel Hill?

>   TECH
>   Good guess. 114 Beechwood Ave.

And that is the exact address on OSKANA's personal file.

>   CARTER
>   Let's get someone to knock down a
>   door for us.

EXT. STREET - MORNING

A TRANSIT BUS ROARS AWAY, Ryan crosses the street, removing a pair of sunglasses.

He approaches a house, checking the address he wrote down.

He knocks on the door- no one answers.

BACK YARD

He moves around the house, keeping his head low. He tries the back door- locked. He SHOULDERS IT IN-

The door flings open into the house's

KITCHEN

Where the LANDLORD, an older man, sits at the kitchen table, a phone in his one hand, a SNUB-NOSED SIX-SHOT IN THE OTHER.

Ryan freezes, the gun aimed directly at him.

> LANDLORD
> (to phone operator)
> Yes, can you put me through to the
> police...

Ryan holds his hands up, trying to negotiate his way out.

> RYAN
> Sir, my name is Ryan Taylor-

> LANDLORD
> I know who you are. You're guy who
> betrayed our country. You're the soldier
> who bombed that building.

> RYAN

Sir, please. Let me explain.

> LANDLORD
> The media should send you a thank you
> card. They're thrilled it was one of us...

Ryan sees a picture of the landlord, on the wall, much younger- a SOLDIER IN WORLD WAR II.

> RYAN
> Then you should know... they don't
> know what they're talking about.

The landlord GETS A BUSY signal, re-dials. Ryan holds up Oskana's picture that he printed out.

> RYAN
> Oskana Rowan- this girl rents an
> apartment from you. She is the one
> who gave me the number to detonate
> that bomb. I'm being set up.

The landlord continues to get a busy signal and continues to re-dial.

> RYAN
> ...I need her information if I'm to find
> the people actually responsible for this.

The landlord continues to re-dial.

> RYAN
> And clear my name.

On the news, the BROADCASTERS continue to bash RYAN... blaming his military training, and as such, blaming the military for the bombing.

RYAN
Please... you know as well as I do...

Finally the 911 OPERATOR ANSWERS. But the landlord
says nothing.

RYAN
...Our military does not create traitors...

A tense moment. The landlord reluctantly making a leap of
faith... He HANGS UP.

LANDLORD
Then it'll be up to you to prove that...

Uncaulks the gun.

INT. LANDLORD'S HOUSE - LATER

Ryan follows the landlord into his

OFFICE

LANDLORD
Why don't you let the police pick you
up? They would believe you.

RYAN
We don't have that kind of time.
Besides, finding the girl only proves I'm
an accomplice. I have to give them guy
in the mask.

LANDLORD
And how will my records help you?

RYAN
I can follow the money.

The landlord pulls Oskana's file... and he sees a number of recipts.

> LANDLORD
> But she only ever paid in cash.

INT. CARTER'S SUV - SAME

His agents load their weapons, readying for a raid. The speaker on the cell SQUAWKS

> SPEAKER (V.O.)
> OK guys, we got a judge to sign off on
> the warrant and you'll have full
> cooperation of the PPD.

INT. LANDLORD'S HOUSE - OFFICE - SAME

Ryan sits, reading through Oskana's RENTAL AGREEMENT.

His eyes scanning through fields "Driver's License," "Credit Card Number"- all of them have "Not Available" scribbled in them.

Frustrated.

> LANDLORD
> Let the police pick you up. I'm sure
> they'll believe you.

> RYAN
> Having her information only proves
> she's an accomplice. I need the man in
> the mask. The man on TV.

(NOTE--This dialogue right here is a repeat, and I'm not sure if it works here or before...)

Ryan turns the page and sees a field labeled "REFERENCES..."

There's only one: "ART BOYD," and listed is his home address, phone number.

Ryan picks up the man's phone, setting the page down. Dials the man's number.

The landlord picks up the form.

                    LANDLORD
          I forgot about the references...
               (looking closer)
          Hey, wait a second...

Ryan GETS THE VOICEMAIL. Hangs up.

                    LANDLORD
          Look.

He pulls out another file from Oskana's folder...

                    LANDLORD
          Same name's on the cosigner lease.

He holds up a COSIGNER lease.

                    RYAN
          You think it's real?

                    LANDLORD
          Oh, I check them all out.

But he looks as if he's remembering the name... He types something into his computer. Hits "ENTER."

                    LANDLORD
          See that.
               (points to the screen)
          He's a popular guy apparently.

There's a list of ten names that filter up...

> LANDLORD
> And they all came to me around the
> same time last summer.

Ryan squints at the names.

> LANDLORD
> Oskana, YAKOV!, Omar, Victor- Any
> of those your guy?

Ryan prints out the list.

Then- POUNDING AT THE DOOR.

> LANDLORD
> (calling down hall at
> door)
> Yes?

> POLICE OFFICER (O.S.)
> Pittsburgh Police, sir. Can you open
> up?

Ryan takes the list of terrorist names out of the printer.

> RYAN
> They traced the girl's address to you.

Ryan takes the piece of paper, and the landlord ushers Ryan toward the back of the house. The officer keeps KNOCKING. The landlord goes to the door, but stops.

> LANDLORD
> Hey.

Ryan turns.

> LANDLORD
> (getting one last
> chance to say it)
> Go get em'.

Ryan smirks, turns and leaves.

EXT. LARA'S APARTMENT COMPLEX - MORNING

Squirrel Hill apartments. Tight streets. Suburbans arrive, along with police. An OFFICER approaches Carter-

> OFFICER
> The neighbors say they haven't seen
> anyone all day. Our guys checked the
> entry points and there's no explosives so
> far as we can tell.

INT. JEEP - MOVING TOWARD GROUND ZERO - SAME

OSKANA drives, three other men sit in the car with her. Yakov, in the passenger seat, loads his gun.

A man sits in shadows in the back.

EXT. GROUND ZERO - MOMENTS LATER

Oskana's jeep arrives. A NATIONAL GUARDSMEN stops her at the checkpoint.

> NATIONAL GUARDSMEN
> Woah, no civilian vehicles!

Oskana flashes her KDTA TV MEDIA PASS.

> OSKANA
> We're with the media.

She smiles.

> OSKANA
> ...here to shoot the president.

The national guardsman looks in the back of the jeep- the one terrorist holding up his camera. He checks over her badge.

> NATIONAL GUARDSMEN
> OK- but park over there.

Oskana gives him a wink and pulls INTO GROUND ZERO.

EXT. GROUND ZERO - MOMENTS LATER

Oskana pulls up. She dumps her media pass, readies a GLOCK, stuffs it in back of her pants.

The other terrorists exit- they put on fire fighters and FEMA worker outfits...

EXT. ART BOYD'S HOUSE - DRIVEWAY - SAME

Ryan observes the nice, upscale home from a far. Sees ART BOYD packing up his car, luggage and bags. Ryan holsters his gun.

Heads down to the

DRIVEWAY

Art emerges with a bag of luggage.

> RYAN
> Excuse me, are you Art Boyd?

                    ART
    I'm sorry, this is private property.

                    RYAN
    Ah, yes, but your office said I could find
    you here.

                    ART
    You're on private property and I will call
    the police.

Ryan brandishes the cosigner agreements.

                    RYAN
    Did you co-sign these documents?

Art can't help but take a glance of them for a second, knows he's
caught-

                    ART
        That's it.

He heads back into the house to call the police, shuts the door-

RYAN KICKS IN THE DOOR, pulling his GLOCK.

                    RYAN
    Get away from the phone.

                    ART
    Jesus Christ, please, please don't kill
    me.

                    RYAN
    Why did you sign these?
        (flashes the papers at
        him)

ART

Just put down the gun-

RYAN

Oskana Rowan, Yakov Dmitry! Why
did you sign these!?

Art sweats, terrified... but more so of the secrets he's holding.

ART

They needed a front-man.

RYAN

For what?

ART

To be a co-signer, leases, loans; vouch
for them, find them jobs- just look the
other way.

RYAN

From what?

ART

From their money.

Ryan, realizing something...

ART

Someone to cover whatever it was they
were doing- suspicious transactions,
unusual wire transfers-

RYAN

You're their banker.

ART

Banker, lliason. I'm in charge of their

money account.

RYAN

Why you?

ART
(nodding, already
trying to defend
himself)
The Zurich branch of my bank put
them in touch with me- I thought they
were just a couple of Saudi migrants
trying to avoid taxes, it happens all the
time!

Ryan throws the rental agreements at him-

RYAN
They're god-damned terrorists!

ART

ART
You have to understand- the initial
deposit in the account checked out! I
was just tasked to manage it!

RYAN
How much do they have?

ART

25 Million.

A beat.

RYAN
I need into that account.

ART

No.

RYAN

Understand- getting into that account
is the only way I can track this guy's
location.

ART

They've been watching me! They've got
my internet connection, they're
monitoring my accounts, my cell
phone. They'll know if I show anyone!
They'll kill me.

RYAN

Finding this group's leader is the only
chance I have of making it through the
day.

ART

Look, I know everything about these
men, and I know you weren't a part of
their plans. I can clear you with the
FBI.

RYAN

It has to be their leader, the guy
speaking for them.

ART

I can verify your innocence!

RYAN

The leader is the only one people will
listen to.

                    ART
         It's not time!

Beat. Ryan is taken by that.

                    RYAN
         For what?

                    ART
         Please. I just need a few more minutes.

                    RYAN
         Time for what!?

                    ART
         To release the account.

                    RYAN
         To whom?

Art gulps...

                    ART
         The media.

Beat.

                    RYAN
         Why?

                    ART
         There's... going to be a second attack...

BANG! Out of nowhere, the window shatters and a bullet tears
through Art's neck. AN AMBUSH! Ryan drops to the floor.
More gunfire.

Looks out the window. Sees, far away, a SNIPER crouched in

this bushes- BANG! Ryan yanks away as another shot tears through the window. He caulks his gun.

Art GASPS, trying to say something.

Ryan goes over... tries listening...

> RYAN
> I have to find their leader...

> ART
> Mikel...

Ryan tries listening.

> ART
> (barely audible)
> Mikel Razanov.

This name strikes Ryan.

EXT. OUTSIDE ART'S HOME - SAME

The sniper, a tall, brutish guy, tries scoping out Ryan, but can't find him. Gritting his teeth. He triggers his mic.

> SNIPER
> Razanov.

> RAZANOV (V.O.)
> Yes.

> SNIPER
> I had to kill the banker.

INTERCUT WITH RAZANOV

> RAZANOV (V.O.)
> Why? There was only a few more

minutes left!

SNIPER
It's the American. He's here.

Razanov pauses.

RAZANOV
Ivan... it is crucial to the our plan that
the bank account is released to the
media.

SNIPER
No sweat.

WHAM! From out of nowhere, Ryan slams the sniper.
Knocking him over. Ryan caulks his gun, jams it in the man's
face.

RYAN
Where is Razanov!?

SNIPER
You think you can stop this!

RYAN
Where is he!?

SNIPER
But Al-Fahad is so much stronger than
you believe.

Ryan SHOOTS THE SNIPER IN THE KNEECAP. Sniper
reacts with violent pain. Ryan jams the gun in his face.

RYAN
Give me his location!

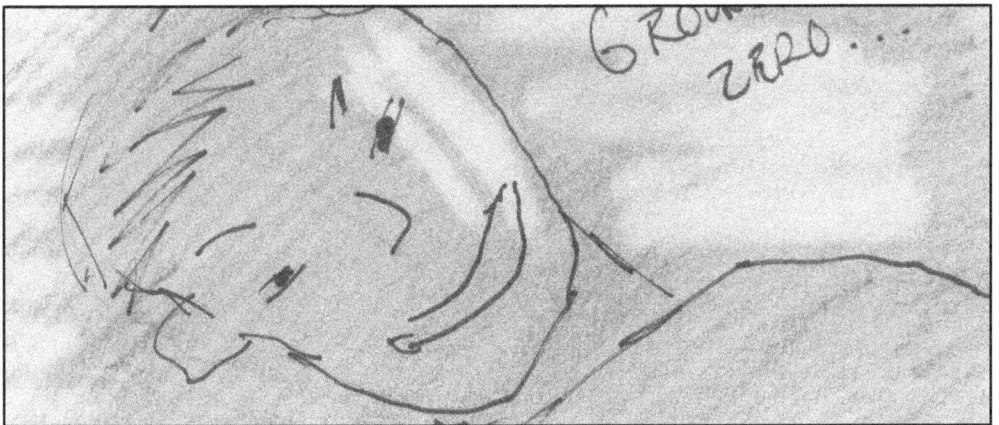

The sniper recovers from the pain, eyes rolling. Ryan grabs the man's collar.

                    RYAN
          Where?

The sniper looks Ryan in the eye... and smiles.

                    SNIPER
          Ground Zero.

It suddenly hits Ryan.

EXT. GROUND ZERO - SAME

The president shakes hands of relief workers. Cheering. Chanting: "USA! USA! USA!"

Oskana lurks in the background, revealing a sharp blade at her hip...

EXT. ART'S HOUSE - SAME

Ryan, on the phone. Frantic.

                    BUREAUCRAT (V.O.)
          Federal Bureau of Investigation, how
          may I-

                    RYAN
          Yes, I need you to put me through to an
          agent Carter.

INTERCUT WITH BUREAUCRAT IN DC, sitting there, eating Bonbons.

                    BUREAUCRAT
          OK, well all potential information is

currently being routed through the
bureau's intelligence office in Quantico-

> RYAN
> I have intel on an imminent attack.

> BUREAUCRAT
> Yes, but we are currently overloaded
> with tips from many-

> RYAN
> Lady, this isn't a tip! They're getting
> ready to attack again!

> BUREAUCRAT
> Sir, I am a respected member of the
> FBI and I am not to be called "lady."

> RYAN
> Jesus Christ!
> (beat, taking the
> plunge)
> I'm the man who bombed the Snyder
> building!

An SUV suddenly screeches up behind him- backup. A
TERRORIST emerges, firing. Ryan leaps out of the way.

INT. OSKANA'S HOUSE - SAME

SWAT break the door down, rushing in, weapons out, strafing
around the corners. Barking orders.

Carter follows them in, looking around the apartment. He sees a
camera on a tripod connected to a pile of servers... CLICKING,
WHIRLING AWAY. And a computer.

CARTER
Look for anything about the next
target.

EXT. ART'S HOUSE - SAME

Terrorists, unloading from the SUV, loading their machine guns,
spreading out. Here are a few names so we can differ them-
GRUSHA, a real mean looking woman equipped with an assault
rifle. Three terrorists and a GEEK who is there to do tech work.

GRUSHA
He got Ivan!
(to Geek)
Check to see that the account info has
been sent!

The geek rushes off to the house. The terrorists surround the
forest outlying Art's house.

GRUSHA
(to her men)
And the American doesn't get away.

FURTHER AWAY, BEHIND TREE

Ryan, still on the phone.

RYAN
(whispering)
I need to speak with special agent Ron
Carter. I am the terrorist who blew up
the Snyder building and I am looking to
confess my crimes.

BANG! Tree bark explodes by his ear. He yanks away and into
battle formation, gun out, shooting back.

INT. OSKANA'S APARTMENT - SAME

Carter, searching through the house, seeing all of the evidence that Oskana was in fact involved. A DETECTIVE relishes.

> DETECTIVE
> Oh, we got these guys by the balls now!

INT. ART'S HOUSE - SAME

The geek enters, searching for Art's dead body. Finds it. Pats it down. Nothing.

> GEEK
> Razanov said it would be on him!

> GRUSHA (V.O.)
> Keep searching!

EXT. WOODS OUTSIDE ART'S HOUSE - SAME

BANG! BANG! BANG! World War III. Ryan, running through the woods, faced with an onslaught of terrorists wielding machine guns. Still on the phone ("ON HOLD" muzak playing), he fires back.

INT. OSKANA'S APARTMENT - SAME

Carter's men hook wires into her computer, slam up their own laptop. Breaking in.

> TECH
> C'mon baby, Daddy needs a new pair of
> shoes!

EXT. WOODS - SAME

A terrorist approaches... gun raised... passes a tree...

BAM, RYAN APPEARS AND SMASHES HIM IN THE FACE. Knocking him to the ground. Blood gushes around the man's face- dead.

He picks up the man's machine gun. Firing back. He keeps dialing through all of this chaos.

INT. OSKANA'S APARTMENT - SAME

The tech types something in the laptop-

> TECH
> This baby'll rip down any firewall she's
> got on here.

Click. A LOADING BAR appears, starting at 0% percent.

Carter hangs over head.

> CARTER
> Good. Good.

Another tech approaches him with a phone.

> CARTER
> Agent Carter, some guys' trying to get
> through to you.

Carter accepts the phone. He HEARS THE GUNFIRE IMMEDIATELY.

EXT. WOODS - SAME

Ryan, ducking from gunfire, firing back.

> CARTER (V.O.)
> Hello!?

> RYAN

Carter! Carter! Listen!

                    CARTER (V.O.)
Ryan?

                    RYAN
Listen to me. The secondary target is-

BANG! Ryan drops the phone.

                    CARTER (V.O.)
Ryan!?

Ryan shoots back, picking it up. STATIC INVADES THE
PHONE SIGNAL.

                    RYAN
The secondary target is...

CARTER

He tries hearing through the STATIC.

                    CARTER
I can't hear you!

                    RYAN
...res...nt...

                    CARTER
Ryan! I'm losing you!

                    RYAN
THE PRESIDENT!

Then, it hits Carter. The CALL DIES. He looks up at the
maps on the wall, the pictures of the Snyder building...

...and then the television playing news footage of GROUND

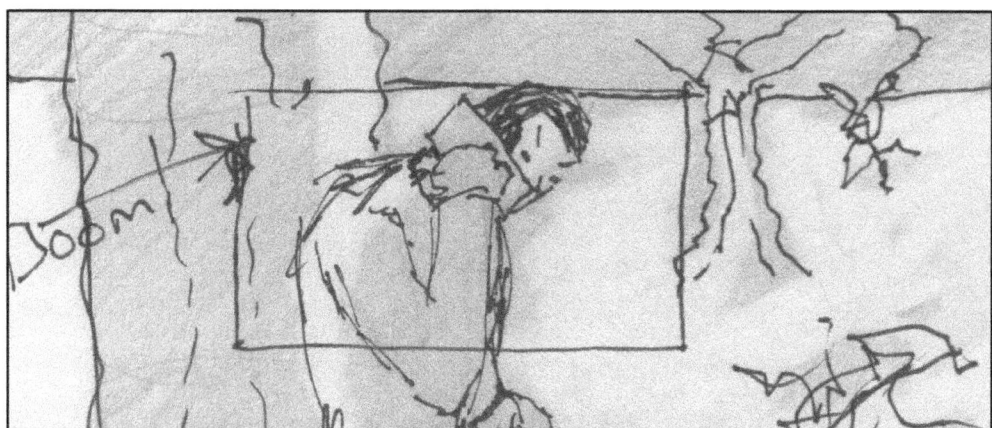

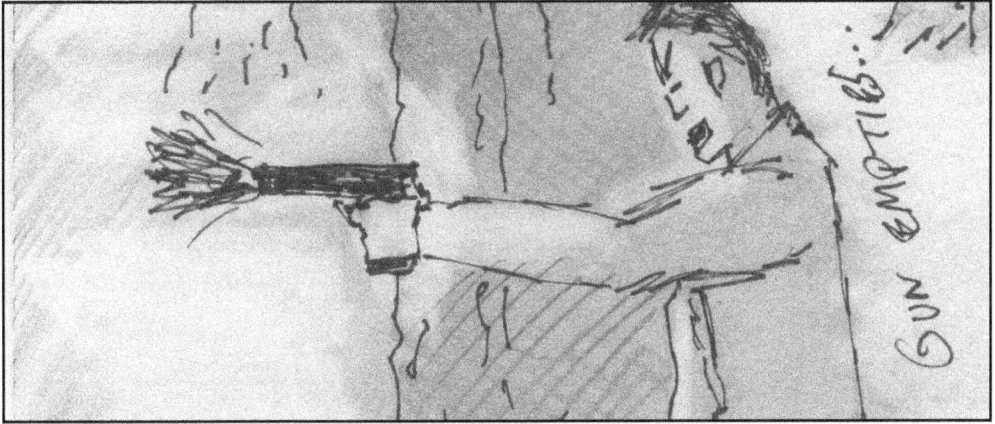

ZERO...and the president SHAKING HANDS!

With horror:

>CARTER
>(to an agent)
>Get me the secret service!

RYAN

>RYAN
>Carter!

Suddenly, Ryan is bashed on the head by Grusha. He crumples to the ground, dazed. She secures his arm.

>GRUSHA
>(to other terrorist)
>Get his other arm. Move!

They both pick him up... and begin dragging him back toward Art's house.

CARTER

Rushing through the halls of the apartment, racing down the stairwell.

>CARTER
>Then get me a section chief!

OSKANA'S APARTMENT

The tech, still trying to break in, the loading bar reaching 50%...

>TECH
>Lay down for me, baby.

RYAN

Grusha and the terrorist drag him into Art's house.

CARTER

Trying to get through, almost hysterical.

INT. ART'S HOUSE - LIVING ROOM

Ryan begins coming back to consciousness. The Geek returns with an iPAD.

> GEEK
>
> I found it!

> GRUSHA
>
> Then send it.

> GEEK
>
> But he didn't write anything yet.

> GRUSHA
>
> Then make up something!

Grusha locks herself behind Ryan, wrapping her arms beneath his, then clasping her hands behind his neck. He comes back to consciousness, thrashing, but trapped in this stance.

> GRUSHA
> (to other terrorist)
> DO IT!

The other terrorist kneels, grabs Ryan's gun, places it in his hand, forcing the grip closed. Ryan struggles against them both. They are forcing him to commit suicide.

The Geek types away on the iPAD.

> GEEK

>   (reading as he types)
>   ...I feel so guilty, but I was too afraid to
>   do anything...until now...I can no
>   longer fear death...can no longer betray
>   my country...

Ryan still struggles with the gun, Grusha still holds him tight.
Both gritting, grunting. The terrorist struggling to push down on
Ryan's grip.

EXT. GROUND ZERO - SAME

The president, still shaking hands, pumping them up.

>   PRESIDENT
>   We'll get em'. Trust me. They'll hear
>   from all of us!

INT. ART'S HOUSE - SAME

Ryan, giving it his all to keep the gun from being pressed toward
his head... screaming.

The Geek finishes up his typing.

>   GEEK
>   (reading)
>   ...I have included an attachment that
>   will assist you greatly. Done.

>   GRUSHA
>   Send it!

Then- the Geek hits SEND- the data bar LOADS SUPER
FAST.

EXT. OSKANA'S APARTMENT COMPLEX - SAME

Carter, finally on the line with secret service.

> CARTER
>
> I don't have time to explain, you just
> have to pull him out of there!

> SECTION CHEIF (V.O.)
> He's getting ready to speak!

EXT. GROUND ZERO - SAME

The president, smiling. Yakov appears before him, dressed as a fireman, extending his hand for a shake.

> YAKOV
> Hopefully sooner than you think!

Yakov clutches the president's hand- THEN SUDDENLY REVEALS A GLOCK. In a second he has the Glock pressed to the president' temple, holding him hostage.

Oskana and the other terrorists slit the secret service men's throats. They drop, lifeless.

INT. OSKANA'S APARTMENT - SAME

The tech, watching the loading bar almost reach...

BINGO! 100%.

> TECH
> I am a God.

But what he doesn't see... is inside the computer itself... a stack of C-4, the light shifting from red... TO GREEN. BEEP!

> TECH
> (warming his hands)

C'mon my sweet little baby, give me
everything.

Hits the space bar. BOOM! A white flash.

CARTER - OUTSIDE

Carter, hysterical-

                    CARTER
          It wasn't a terrorist attack! It was just
          bai-

SUDDENLY, everything behind him explodes! A fireball
erupts. Knocking him face first into the grass.

EXT. GROUND ZERO - SAME

Yakov holds the president hostage. Recuse workers and fire
fighters freeze in terror.

                    YAKOV
          DON'T MOVE! NONE OF YOU!

INT. ART'S HOUSE - SAME

Ryan, STILL struggling against the lowering gun, sees on TV
this happen. He reacts by SMASHING THE BACK OF HIS
HEAD INTO GRUSHEL'S FACE; her nose instantly
explodes with blood.

Then, still resisting the gun, wraps himself into the terrorist,
grabbing his arm, using the gun to shoot Grushel. Then, raising
the gun, right into the terrorist' JOWEL-

BANG! Blood explodes.

The geek tries unholstering his weapon, but Ryan gets him

before he can. BANG! BANG!

EXT. GROUND ZERO - SAME

A relief worker, stepping forward, mask attached to his face.

> RELIEF WORKER
> Yessss! Ladies and gentlemen! Calm
> down! I just wanted to thank you...

He rips off the mask, revealing that it is Razanov-

> RAZANOV
> ...for cleaning up my mess!

INT. ART'S HOUSE - SAME

Ryan, watching this in horror.

EXT. OSKANA'S APARTMENT COMPLEX - SAME

Carter, crawling through the ground. Dazed.

EXT. GROUND ZERO - SAME

The president, still held hostage. Watching... terrified...

> RAZANOV
> ...as well, an even bigger thank you in
> advanced...for cleaning up today's.

Razanov has a cell phone out- he hits SEND- BOOOOOM!!!

An explosion rips through the area.

INT. ART'S HOUSE - SAME

Ryan, his eyes saucering in terror as he sees Razanov hitting
SEND on the news- and then the live feed FRITZES. Knocked
out. Killed.

RYAN
No!

Ryan almost drops right to his knees.

EXT. OSKANA'S APARTMENT COMPLEX - SAME

Carter, crawling through the grass. Covered in soot. Singed.
His radio crackles.

RADIO
Sir! Sir! They just hit Ground Zero!

Carter, even dazed, can't help but lower his head in shame.

His men race over and help him, pull him away from the fire.

INT. ART'S HOUSE - SAME

Ryan, still watching the TV screen- the image has cut back to
the anchors in the studio, all of them taken off guard.

ANCHOR
We're not, exactly sure what has just
happened- we've lost contact with our
field reporter.

Ryan drops to his knees, knowing that the president has been
killed.

ANCHOR #1
I'm getting reports of chaos down at the
Snyder building now.

EXT. OSKANA'S APARTMENT COMPLEX - SAME

Carter, still ashamed. Listening to the radio.

RADIO (V.O.)

...the president is unaccounted for...I
dont know, it was a pretty big blast...

Carter dials his phone. Bannings ANSWERS.

CARTER
Do the satellites show anything?

BANNINGS (V.O.)
The explosion clouded their view.

Carter's head drops.

BANNINGS (V.O.)
How about the girl's apartment? Any
leads.

Carter just looks at the blaze...

INT. ART'S HOUSE - SAME

Ryan, still devastated. On his knees.

Then, BEEPING from the iPAD- Ryan looks at it. It says...
"E-MAIL SENT"

Ryan pulls it up- and it reveals the bank account Art was
guarding. Numbers, descriptions of transactions, hundreds of
them.

And it has been sent to a LONG LIST OF JOURNALISTS IN
THE MEDIA: CXN, VOX, NBC, MSNBC...

On Grusha's belt, her radio CRACKLES.

RAZANOV
Has the account been sent?

Ryan looks over, peaked by the voice.

> RAZANOV (V.O.)
> Grusha, come in. Has the account
> been sent?

Ryan picks up the radio.

> RYAN
> Why do you want the media to see your
> finances?

Intercut with Razanov, who reacts with surprise.

> RAZANOV
> Maybe there is still more to come.

Ryan, a beat.

> RYAN
> You set me up...

> RAZANOV
> We needed someone to distract the
> authorities.

> RYAN
> Why me...?

> RAZANOV
> Because you thought you could just
> walk away...

Ryan is stopped by this. The words triggering a revelation...

> RAZANOV
> ...from your jihad.

Ryan, slowly being pulled back into a nightmare...

RYAN
Your brothers wanted me to bomb an
American embassay.

RAZANOV
We needed to know if your hatred was
true...

RYAN
And I gave you my word.

RAZANOV
But not your life!

Ryan... the words stabbing deep.

RYAN
You don't need that anymore.

RAZANOV
You abandoned your destiny, Mr.
Taylor.

RYAN
I wasn't going to commit suicide to
prove my loyalty.

RAZANOV
And so... this will be your living Hell.

Ryan, gritting his teeth.

RYAN
Listen. I only want you to tell them: I
had nothing to do with this.

RAZANOV
Why would I risk my crediblity for a

coward?

Ryan grits his teeth, hearing the word "coward."

RYAN
The police are going to kill me!

A terrorist notifies Razanov that the file has been sent.

RAZANOV
Then consider it your sacrifice.

CLICK. The radio GOES DEAD.

Ryan grits his teeth. Pissed for supplicating to the terrorist mastermind, despaired at still being stuck in all of this.

He looks over at the banker's IPAD... the account.

ON RAZANOV

He smiles, looks over at...

The president... now unconscious, laid up on a stretcher.

ON RYAN

Thumbing through the accounts...

Then, FAINT POLICE SIRENS FADE UP IN THE DISTANCE. The police, arriving.

OUTSIDE

With the iPAD clutched in his hands, he races out to the terrorist's SUV, gets in, shuts the door, and peels out of there...

EXT. ALLEY - LATER

Carter sits on the curb, oxygen mask pressed to his face,

despondent. The aftermath of an explosion all around him- fire trucks, cops, EMTs. His phone RINGS. He answers.

> RYAN (V.O.)
> His names Mikel Razanov! The guy at
> Ground Zero is Mikel Razanov. He's
> their leader. You have to get in touch
> with the media- he sent them his bank
> account.
> (hears no reply)
> Carter?

INTERCUT WITH RYAN DRIVING, CHECKING THE iPAD.

But Carter doesn't react to in the information. Instead-

> CARTER
> Why did the CIA want to make a deal
> with you?

Ryan, caught off guard by the question.

> RYAN
> I'm sorry?

> CARTER
> What made your silence so valuable to
> them?

Ryan doesn't want to go into it... too painful.

> RYAN
> They didn't want people to know... that
> they'd already made a deal with me
> once before.

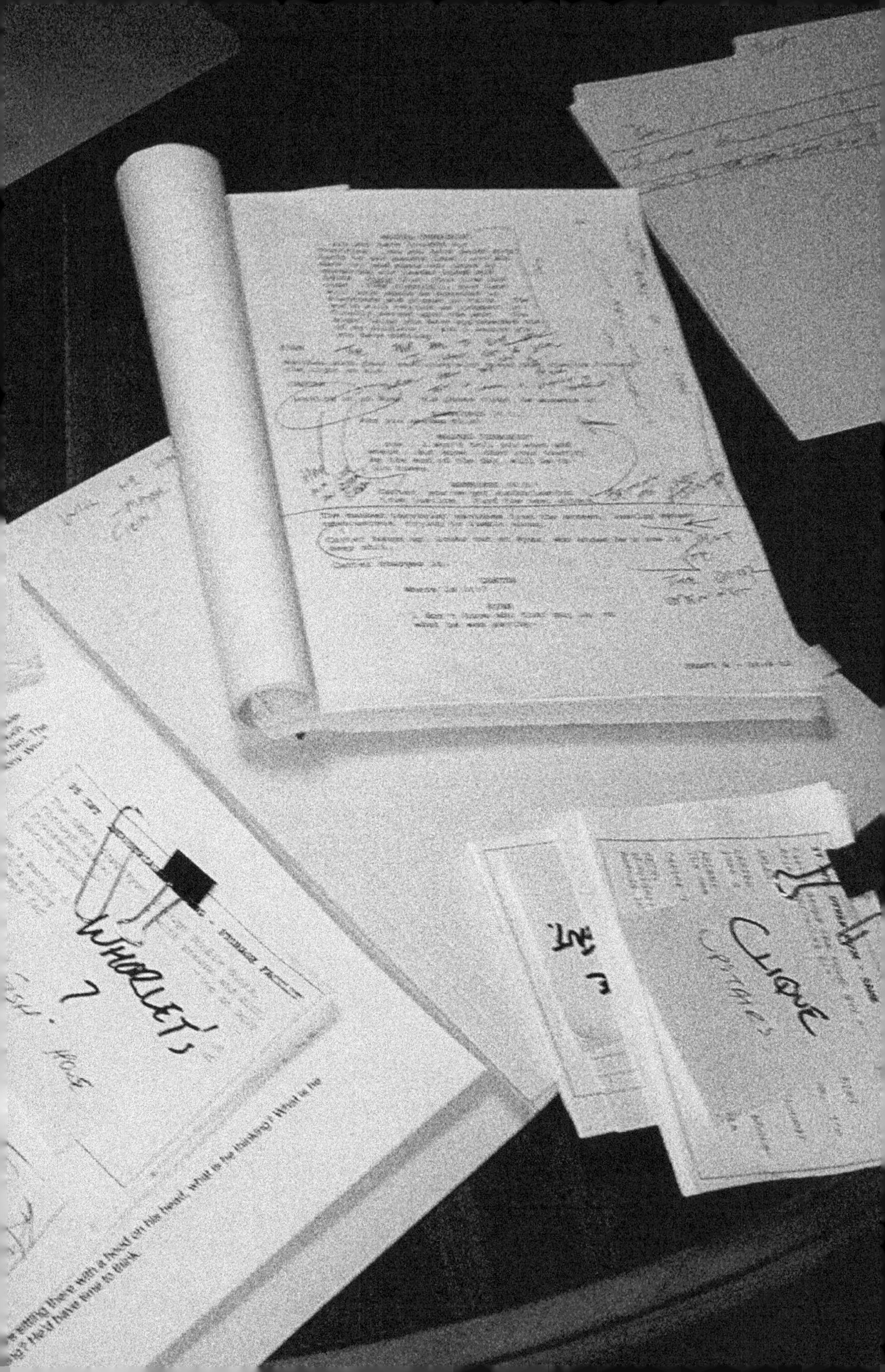
CLIQUE

Getting ready to film a scene.

Something catches Carter's attention on TV: A news report about Ryan...

                    ANCHOR #1 (V.O.)
          ...was just spotted leaving the scene of a
          brutal slaying. 5 dead including a well
          respected, Pittsburgh banker...

Carter, considering what Ryan just said, combined with he's just learned from the news...

                    CARTER
          My teams gone, Ryan.

Ryan stops. Hearing the morbid tone.

                    CARTER
          Cops, techs, SWAT. They're all dead.
               (beat)
          The place you sent us to was
          boobytrapped.

                    RYAN
               (searching for words)
          I didn't know. Carter...

                    CARTER
          Another bomb detonated, and now
          more men are dead.

Ryan, guilt cascading over his face.

                    CARTER
          My only regret now, of course... is that
          I didn't kill you sooner.

                    RYAN

Carter.

CARTER

Yes?

RYAN

This isn't over.
(beat)
He's targeting the city next.

Carter hangs up the phone.

INT. WAREHOUSE - LATER

Dank. Dark. Miserable. The terrorists drag the president in out of the daylight.

They SIT HIM DOWN IN A CHAIR. A terrorist readies something in the background, a tool of some kind.

PRESIDENT
(scared)
You think they're not going to find me?
I'm the president of the United States.

RAZANOV
Don't worry, "Mr. President." There
was so much confusion back there, it'll
take them a while before they start
looking.

PRESIDENT
Whatever you want... they won't give it
to you: the United States does not
negotiate with terrorists.

The president looks Razanov in the eyes, seeing the eyes of the devil...

                    RAZANOV
          Ah... but Mr. President...

A terrorist WHIRLS A DRILL IN THE BACKGROUND.
The other terrorists grab the president, holding him down. The
president thrashes. Terrified.

                    RAZANOV
          This is not a negotiation.

Razanov walks off into the darkness as the president
SCREAMS!

EXT. BACK ALLEY - AFTERNOON

A TECH moves Carter to the back of their SUV, opening the
tailgate, using it to sit a laptop playing the news.

                    TECH
          All of Al Fahad's financial purchases,
          transactions, right here in a numbered
          Swiss bank account.

                    CARTER
          How did the media get it so fast?

                    TECH
          A banker sent it out. Poor bastard- Al-
          Fahad sent six guys after him!

The tech pulls up the account on the laptop.

                    CARTER
          Why wouldn't he send it to us though?

The tech shrugs-

                    TECH
        We got everything on these guys.

Carter looks down at the screen. Amidst all the transactions, he
sees one that catches his eyes: $2 million dollars...

                    CARTER
        What's this?

The tech looks.

                    TECH
        Uhhmm, 2 million; a transaction that
        occurred August 14th, 2011...
        in....Moscow.

                    CARTER
        What is it?

                    TECH
        Doesn't say... but...

He reads up on the account, sees the next transaction was for a
shipping company.

                    TECH
        The next purchase was placement on a
        freighter company based out of
        Khazakstan. Whatever it was...

He continues to type...

                    TECH
        It took quite a trip. Caspian to Iran,
        then another freighter through the
        South Atlantic...

Carter watches the tech click through the shipping manifests.

                    TECH
Where it bounced around in South
America for a few months.

                    CARTER
They're using the traffiking lanes.

                    TECH
For what?

                    CARTER
Get me information on a Mikel
Razanov.

EXT. INDUSTRIAL PLANT - LATER

A sprawling complex of rust and warehouses. Ryan roars up in
the S.U.V. Exits. Goes to the back tailgate, opens it. Searches
through and finds...

A number of armory boxes... some C-4... and a machine gun.
He arms himself with it.

EXT. CARTER - SAME

Carter, clicking away on laptops, gets a call. Answers.

                    BANNIGNS (V.O.)
We confirmed the swiss bank account
belongs to the name you gave us.

                    CARTER
Razanov?

                    BANNIGNS (V.O.)
The transactions gave us a lead too. An
industrial factory in Hyde park.

                    CARTER
          He's going to iniate another attack.

                 BANNINGS (V.O.)
          I'm readying you another tactical unit-

                    CARTER
          Bannings, I think Razanov had a
          weapon shipped into the country.

                 BANNINGS (V.O.)
          This is our only lead. And right now
          it's being flashed up on every news
          outlet in the country. We have to move
          on it before half the country shows up
          there and chases him off.

Carter, beat. Relenting.

INT. INDUSTRIAL PLANT - SAME

Rust bleeding walls. Rotten metal. Ibeam skeletons. A tomb of
a once thriving industry...

Ryan blasts through the door, his G-39c out in front of him, the
gun's flashlight cutting through the blackness.

He maneuvers down miserable corridors that look like something
out of Silent Hill, strafing past leaky pools of darkness...

Turning corners, sticking the G-39c out. Breathing heavy.
Finger on the trigger. The flashlight cutting through like a white
blade.

He comes to a sign on the wall written in blood: "Let Freedom
Ring..."

Ryan rips it down in rage. Suddenly, hears RUSTLING in

another room.

SECONDS LATER

He comes to a door with another sign written in blood: "Save your country..."

He kicks in the door, leading way into a

DARK ROOM

His light slices over a hooded man...sitting in a chair.

> RYAN
> Get up.

The man doesn't move. Ryan, his face perspiring. Fear betraying him.

> RYAN
> You're coming with me... and you're
> going to tell them the truth.
> (beat)
> Razanov!

But the man still doesn't move.

...So Ryan charges over...and yanks down the hood.

His face drops.

It is not a young Razanov... bur rather... a much, much older man.

It is the president.

Yellow utility lights EXPLODE ON, illuminating the terrified man tied to the chair...

His mouth taped. He looks terrified to see Ryan. Ryan removes
the tape.

PRESIDENT

> It's a trap!

Suddenly, behind Ryan, an old television set from the 80s'
FIRES TO LIFE. A grainy image of Razanov, looking into the
camera lens, flashes on.

RAZANOV

> If you are seeing this… it means you
> have followed my calling… and are
> willing to make a choice. While you
> have come here seeking me in the
> name of revenge,
>> (I assure you... I am
>>   not your enemy)
> I offer you a consolation.

Ryan watches the TV… horrified.

RAZANOV

> Before you is a man so timid and meek
> that he knowingly risked his own life so
> he could show the people they have no
> reason to fear.

He is, of course, referring to the president…

RAZANOV

> But I assure you, there is every reason to
> be afraid. Strapped to this man's body
> is a device that has traveled many, many
> miles to be here with us today. Certain
> administrations would like to call it a

weapon of mass destruction I prefer the
term: suitcase nuke.

Ryan sees a suitcase sitting next to the president. He kneels,
sweating, opens it... revealing a binzintine of wires, snaking
around two chrome cylinders... all centered around a digital timer.

The timer already dwindling. Ryan sees an iPAD strapped above
it, playing the map of a GPS.

RAZANOV
I assure you detonation would be
catastrophic, destroying the city, and
making the area very uninhabitable for
a hundred years. But since you were
willing to risk your life in the name of
your country's justice, I am going to
give you a chance to stop it. The timer
on the device before you is programmed
for 30 minutes- but it is not powered by
a battery.

Ryan also sees in the case...a heart monitor, beeping away.

RAZANOV
Rather...it is powered by the beating of
the president's heart.

He notices a cord leading out of the case... up onto an IV
jammed into the president's bloody arm.

RAZANOV
The longer his heart continues to pump
blood, the closer the timer reaches zero.

The president looks terrified. Ryan takes in the message, fear
rising in his mind.

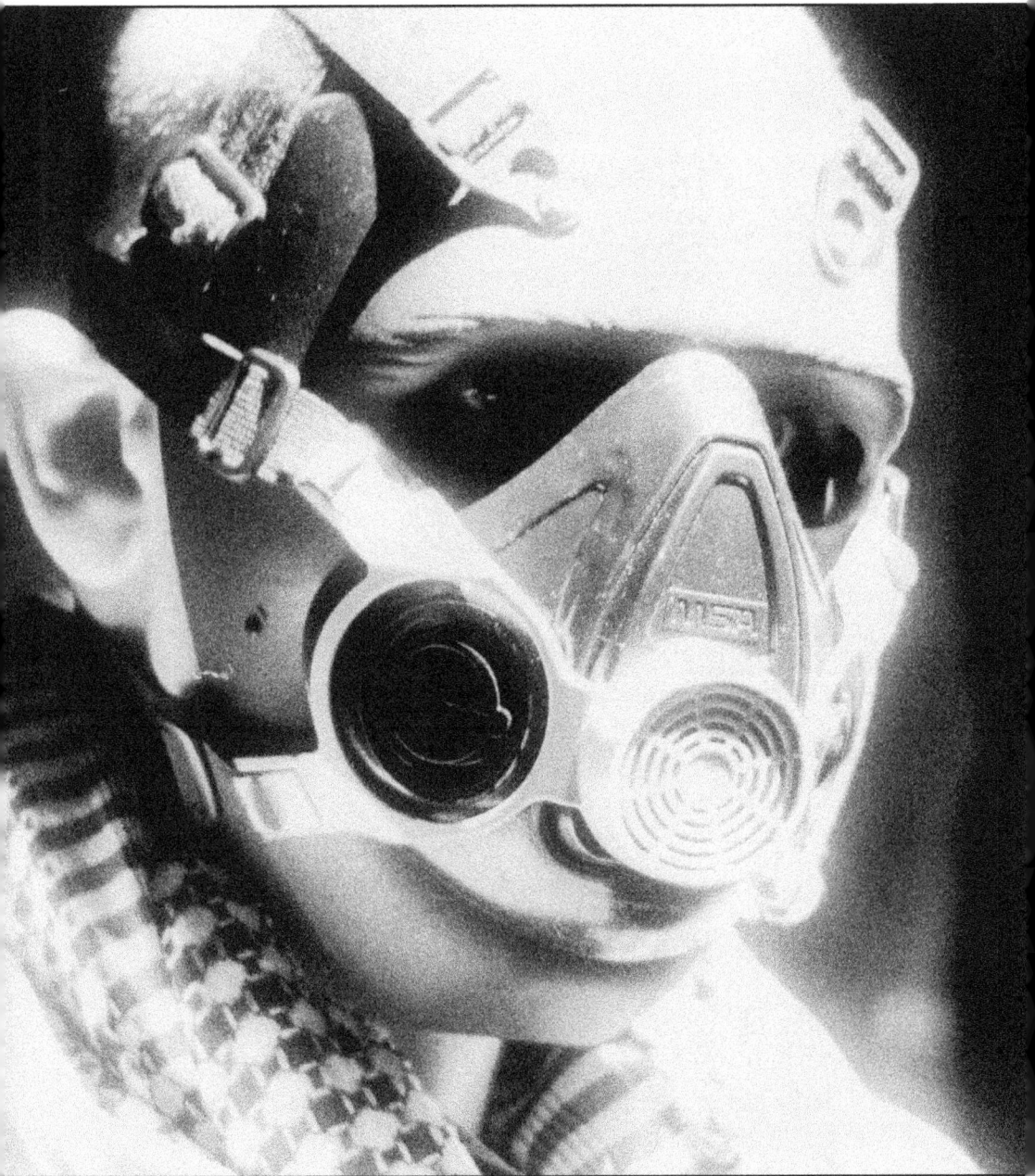

Philip Lewis in character as "Mikel Razanov."

RAZANOV
Trust me: any attempt to remove the
device from the president will result in
immediate detonation. The game is
simple. Kill your leader… save your
country.

RYAN
(realizing, to himself)
That's why he released the account…

He immediately snaps to untying the president.

PRESIDENT
(to Ryan)
Is he telling the truth?

RYAN
Either way- there's going to be hundred
pissed off people here in a matter of
minutes.

RAZANOV
You've come here to exact revenge for
an unspeakable act of evil… but you are
now forced to choose between two
evils. Will you summon the courage to
take a life so that millions might
survive… or will you find that you are
not as courageous as you once believed?

Suddenly, IRATE SCREAMING WAFTS IN FROM
DOWN THE HALLWAY. Ryan listens.

SCREAMS (V.O.)
We're gonna' get you! You son of a

bitch! We're gonna' teach you- you
don't fuck with America, you towel
head!

Ryan frantically rips off the last of the president's restraints.

> PRESIDENT
> What the hell is that?

> RYAN
> Hopefully someone who voted for you.
> C'mon.

He yanks the president out of the chair, helps him up with the
nuke.

He leads the president in another direction.

EXT. INDUSTRIAL WAREHOUSE - MOMENTS LATER

Ryan blasts out a door, the light blinding him. He leads the
president- and the nuke case- outside. Ryan leads him to the car.

> PRESIDENT
> I thought you were with Al Fahad...

> RYAN
> No sir.
> (beat)
> I'm an American.

Puts him in the back.

Ryan gets in, fires the engine up.

The SUV takes off.

INT. CARTER'S SUV - LATER

An agent drives. Arlen, in the back, checks his laptop for information on Razanov.

> ARLEN
> Nothing from the FBI, CIA, or
> Interpol, but we caught a break with the
> FSB.

> CARTER
> Our guy's Russian?

> ARLEN
> Born Mikel S. Razanov, March, 1985,
> in Grozny of the Chechen Republic.
> They only had him in the database
> because of his affiliation with the IIPB.

> CARTER
> So Al Fahad is Chechen?

> ARLEN
> It's a splinter cell.

> CARTER
> Of the IIPB?

> ARLEN
> Al Qadea.

Carter glances back, confused...

> CARTER
> I thought you said he's Chechen.

> ARLEN
> An informant places him leaving Russia
> in the mid 2000s, where he spent the

past seven years moving about the
middle east, working for one of Al
Qadea's higher-ups.

> CARTER
>
> Who?

> ARLEN
> (beat)
> ...Osama Bin Laden.

EXT. HIGHWAY - SAME

Ryan's SUV, screaming past cars. Horns blaring.

INSIDE SUV

Ryan drives frantically. Trying to keep his shit together. In the
back, the nuke timer continues to dwindle.

> RYAN
> Mr. President... I need you to try and
> remember. Did they say anything
> about where they were going?

> PRESIDENT
> No.
> (Regarding the nuke)
> What are we going to do with this?

> RYAN
> But did they mention a location or
> something that might help me find
> them.

> PRESIDENT
> No! They left me in a dark room! Now

what are we going to do about this
thing? There's only 30 minutes left.

Ryan, sweating. Driving.

> PRESIDENT
> I need to call the secret service.

> RYAN
> I'm sorry, sir- the last thing I need is a
> hundred security agents swarming the
> car.

> PRESIDENT
> Then pull over and let me out!

> RYAN
> I can't do that either...

Sweat almost pouring down Ryan's face.

> PRESIDENT
> Why not?

Ryan indicates to the iPAD on the seat next to him... playing
Razanov's video announcing that the president is hooked to a
nuke.

> RYAN
> Razanov had the video sent!

INT. INDUSTRIAL WAREHOUSE - LATER

A SWAT team blasts through the main door, strafing in,
clearing the place. Carter and his men follow in.

Moving down catwalks. Passing through doors.

Curtis and I in Razanov's lair.

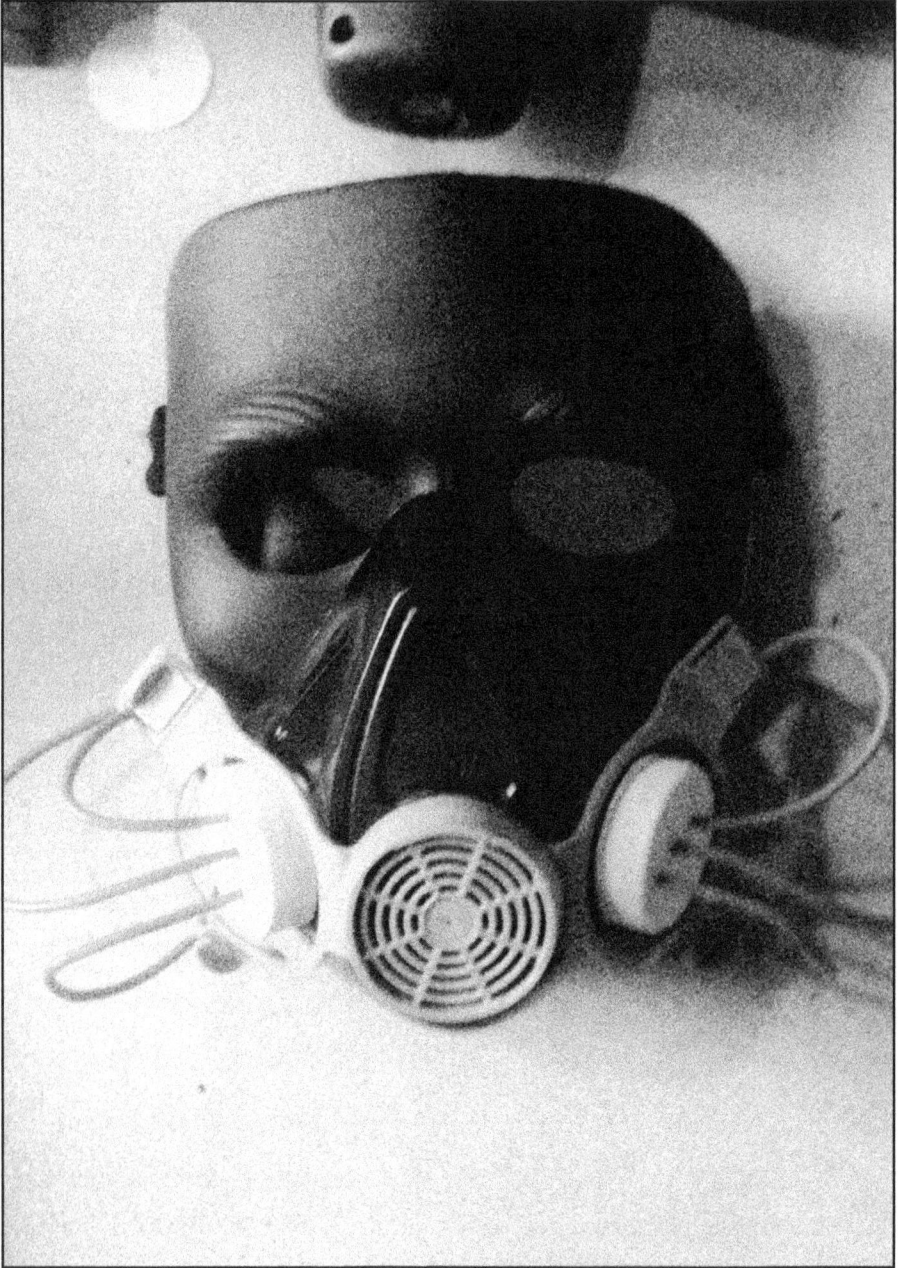

Carter enters the one

ROOM

...where he discovers the chair, the remains of tape scraps, the utility lights- where the president once was. Then, the TV explodes on- Razanov's message about the nuke repeats. Carter looks like someone dying inside.

                    SWAT LEADER
          CLEAR!

He watches, hearing the words "SUITCASE NUKE," "KILL YOUR PRESIDENT."

Then, a tech enters.

                    TECH
          Guy who owns the gas station across
          the street saw Ryan just fifteen minutes
          ago. And he swears he had the
          president with him.

...and if that wasn't even worse news.

INT. RYAN'S SUV - SAME

Ryan, driving frantically through traffic. Like a wide receiver heading for the end zone- but here... there is no end zone.

Ryan's cell rings. He peaks at the display- Carter's number- answers.

                    RYAN
          Yea, I have him.

                    CARTER
          We got you on the security camera

taking him.

RYAN
Don't worry. He's fine.

CARTER
Is it real?

RYAN
I would say so...
(changing topics)
Carter, there's more to this. Razanov's banker didn't send the account to the media- it was Razanov.

CARTER
What?

RYAN
He wanted the people to see his finances. The bomb is not the endgame.

Carter considers this. The timer continues to click.

CARTER
Let me talk to the president.

Ryan hands the phone back to the president.

CARTER (V.O.)
(to President now)
Sir, this is Special Agent Ron Carter, how much time do we have on the clock?

PRESIDENT

29 minutes...

Carter flinches-

> CARTER (V.O.)
> Ok, sir, they're fueling NAOC as we
> speak. Give us your location and we'll
> send a team.

The president starts looking for landmarks, descriptions-

> PRESIDENT
> Uhh, we just got off the, I think it's
> called the parkway, we're on the yel-

Ryan hears this, knows exactly what he's doing, yanks the phone
off him- hangs it up.

WITH CARTER

...Hearing the line go dead.

> CARTER
> (to a tech)
> Get a lock on that phone.

WITH RYAN AND PRESIDENT

The President, worried....

> PRESIDENT
> They'll take this car.

> RYAN
> I can get you to NAOC.

> PRESIDENT
> Those are trusted agents of the United

States government, Ryan.

RYAN
I'm the only one you can trust right
now.

PRESIDENT
Those- My men- took an oath on their
lives to protect me!

RYAN
What makes you think... they're still
your men?

INT. INDUSTRIAL WAREHOUSE - SAME

A nervous Carter, awaiting the phone trace. An agent waits next
to him.

AGENT
Do you think he's going to try and
leverage us?

Carter looks at him, not understanding.

AGENT
With the president.

CARTER
For what?

AGENT
Immunity.

A deadly beat. BEEPING FROM A COMPUTER.

TECH
(re: computer)

We've got him going westbound, 376,
mile marker 15, coordinates 1, 3, 3,
niner!

Carter readies his radio.

                    CARTER
          (to radio)
     Ready units. We have a lock on the
     president.

                    MAN ON RADIO (V.O.)
     Copy. Do we have authorization to
     strike?

Carter, thrown for a loop on that. Confused.

                    CARTER
     Repeat that.

                    MAN ON RADIO (V.O.)
     Is this is a kill, no capture?

                    CARTER
     That's the President of the United
     States, sargent.

                    MAN ON RADIO (V.O.)
     Not anymore...

Carter, paused by this.

                    CARTER
     Come again, sargent.

                    MAN ON RADIO (V.O.)
     Congress just voted him out.

This hits Carter hard.

INT. RYAN'S SUV - SAME

The president... agonizing over the ticking nuke. Ryan... driving, nervous. Both oblivious to what's about to happen...

WIDE SHOT OF THE SUV ON THE HIGHWAY

...sliding along like a bug... DEFT ROARING... A FLAT BLACK APACHE HELICOPTER THAT COULD EASILY BE MISTAKEN FOR A MASSIVE HORNET OBLITERATES OUR VIEW... ROTORS SLICING AT THE SKY... HEADED RIGHT FOR THE SUV.

INSIDE SUV

Ryan hears this. Looks back. Sees the Apache approaching. Something doesn't feel right.

INT. COMMAND CENTER - CORRIDOR - AFTERNOON

Carter hunches in the shadows, cell phone clutched to his ear-

> CARTER
> He's the president of the United States!

> BANNINGS (V.O.)
> And he's strapped to a nuke! The 25th amendment specifically states that when the president is unable to discharge the powers and duties of his office, the vice president shall immediately assume-

> CARTER
> We don't even know if Razanov is

telling the truth about the bomb.

> BANNINGS (V.O.)
> Well, he's convinced congress.

> CARTER
> So what, we just shoot him off the
> road?

> BANNINGS (V.O.)
> Carter- they found the guy in a training
> camp!

Carter is suddenly stopped by this.

> BANNINGS (V.O.)
> Why do you think the CIA was willing
> to cut him a deal yesterday?

Carter... listening...

> CARTER
> I don't understand.

> BANNINGS (V.O.)
> 2008, the guy goes AWOL from his
> company and the CIA finds him
> cozying up with Al Qadea.

> CARTER
> Why didn't they prosecute him then?

> BANNINGS (V.O.)
> Because he gave them intell on a
> terrorist training camp. The guys a sell
> out- both to them... and to us!

Carter, taking this in...

CARTER
Bannings, he hasn't killed him yet.

BANNINGS
Yea. He's leaving that up to
Washington.

Carter, realizing something. Something very bad.

CARTER
What does that mean?

BANNINGS
We don't negotiate with terrorists...

INT. RYAN'S SUV - SAME

The Apache roaring closer, circling the vehicle.

PRESIDENT
(re: Apache)
I told you...

RYAN
I don't think they're here for me...

Watching the blackhawks...

On the radio, the news announces that vice president TERRY O
NEIL is taking the office of the president... The president is
stunned.

Ryan jerks the wheel, peeling onto the off-ramp.

PRESIDENT
Where are you going?

President Collins (Chuck Getty) meeting with president Reagan and VP Bush. NOT photoshopped!

                    RYAN
There's a business district down the
road.

                 PRESIDENT
What's there?

                    RYAN
Other people.
          (looking back at the
            president)
Your men won't risk the collateral
damage!

                 PRESIDENT
They wouldn't do that!

                    RYAN
I'm sorry, Mr. President... But you just
got impeached.

EXT. SUV

The Apache, flying behind, careening past trees and buildings.

APACHE'S POV

A digital screen cascaded in dials and graphs... all centered
around a... GUN SIGHT... searching the screen... locking on
the SUV... Locked on.

BEEP!

The Apache unloads a hellfire missile. It cuts through the air.

Ryan swerves. The missile hits the road, exploding in a ball of
fire.

The president freaks out.

EXT. INTERSECTION - SAME

The SUV screams through, the helicopter chasing not far off.

He calls Carter-

INT. INDUSTRIAL WAREHOUSE - SAME

Carter's phone rings. He answers it quickly-

> RYAN
>
> Get this thing off me! I'm bringing
> him in!

> CARTER
>
> Ryan, you have to give him up!

> RYAN
>
> They'll kill him.

> CARTER
>
> He's not the president anymore!

> RYAN
>
> You and I both know that's a cop-out.
> They're trying to cover their asses.

> CARTER
>
> He's attached to a nuclear bomb!

> RYAN
>
> And we can still stop it.

Carter, conflicted by this.

> CARTER
>
> Right now, the whole country is out for

his head.

                    RYAN
        Which is why we have to keep our's.

Carter takes a breath... thinking... makes a decision.

                    CARTER
        Then we have to get him on a chopper.

                    RYAN
        He leaves the city, the bomb detonates.

Carter... worried at this.

                    RYAN
        Razanov added in a GPS navigator.

...in the suitcase...attached to the roof of the case...an
IPAD...showing the GPS navigation of where they are...

                    RYAN
        He goes airborne, the bomb blows. He
        leaves the coordinates of the city... the
        bomb blows.

Carter grits his teeth. Taking a breath.

                    CARTER
        I'm sending you information on a safe
        house. I'll assemble a team.

Ryan gets the address on his phone.

                    RYAN
        Are these men you can trust?

                    CARTER

Ditch your phone. The strike unit can
only track you by sight.

Ryan hangs up. Looks back at the helicopter. Tosses his phone
out the window.

SHOTS

The helicopter bears down on the SUV. Machine gun fire.

The SUV, screeching all over the road. Chunks of pavement
ripping up as machine gun fire eats through.

Bullet holes star the SUV's back window.

RYAN
GET DOWN!

The president ducks, covering his head. Glass shatters over his
head.

There is a chase.

Ryan decides, at one point, to give the wheel up to the president.

Then he arms himself with the machine gun, firing back at the
helicopter.

Then the machine clicks EMPTY.

Ryan searches through the back- finds a GRENADE
LAUNCHER.

Eventually he is able to draw the helicopter away from the
president, and he takes the chopper down with the grenade
launcher.

We'll cut ahead to when Ryan and the president are back on
foot...

NOTE: Ryan takes a bag with him from the SUV, before it is destroyed- the bag includes weapons, the banker's iPAD, and a vest of c-4.

EXT. ALLEY - LATER

Ryan leads the president through. He checks car after car, looking for one that's unlocked. The nuke continues to countdown toward zero.

Ryan gets frustrated.

> RYAN
> Son of a bitch.

> PRESIDENT
> Here. Allow me.

The president takes Ryan's gun, marches out onto the road an approaching car.

> PRESIDENT
> (to car, AIMING
> THE GUN)
> President of the United States! Get out
> of your car!

The car screeches.

> PRESIDENT
> Move!

The guy gets out. He's on a cell phone.

> GUY
> Holy shit! It's you!
> (to the phone)
> Yea, Becky! You're not gonna' believe

it!

Ryan gets in the driver's side. The president takes the drivers side. They take off.

> GUY
> I think the president just car-jacked me.
> (ALT: I think I just
> got car-jacked by the
> president!)

INT. CAR - SAME

Ryan, driving, hands over the banker's iPAD to the president.

> RYAN
> Look through that account and tell me
> if you see any transaction that leads to a
> location other than the one we were at.

The president looks at it. Thumbing through Razanov's account on the banker's iPAD.

> PRESIDENT
> (reading)
> Ahh... just a cash withdrawal,
> withdrawal, cash, cash- a few
> transactions for other items, but these
> are all cash withdrawals.

Ryan grits his teeth, thinks.

> RYAN
> How about who funded him? What's
> the first deposit?

The president thumbs through the account.

INT. SAFE HOUSE - LATE AFTERNOON

BOMB TECHS unload their gear in the living room. Carter supervises.

> CARTER
> Have your equipment ready; we're not going to have much time once they get here.

The bomb techs unlock PELICAN CASES...

Unroll reams of tools...

INT. CAR - CONTINUOUS

Ryan still drives. The president discovers something in the account.

> PRESIDENT
> Says here, first deposit was made 2011, April - with-
>> (taken a back)
> Wow- 25 million bucks from an AVCO oil.

> RYAN
> Does it say where they're located?

The president looks at them, clicks the address up. He's surprised.

> PRESIDENT
> Hm.

> RYAN
> What?

PRESIDENT
Well it says here... their head office is at
332 Fifth Avenue.

RYAN
Where's that?

PRESIDENT
Ground Zero.

Ryan looks at him.

RYAN
In the Snyder building?

PRESIDENT
Third floor.

This definitely throws Ryan for a loop.

RYAN
Why would they bomb their own
investors?

INT. SAFE HOUSE - CONTINUOUS

Arlen studies his laptop screen.

ARLEN
It's a shell corp.

He signals Carter over to the computer.

CARTER
How do you know?

ARLEN
The majority of their invoices are

advertising and consulting, the website says its publicly traded, but there's no listing of an AVCO oil on the NASDAQ, all of the major wire transfers are through numbered Swiss bank accounts, it's an LLC.

He is looking at Razanov's financial account.

> CARTER
> Can we trace the DBA?

Arlen types into his laptop. Windows flash around on his screen.

> ARLEN
> I can't find a name... but it says the
> papers were filed in...
>> (stops, confused)
> The head office is here, but the DBA
> was filed in... Virginia.

A beat.

> CARTER
> Where?

Arlen looks up at him, his face white.

> ARLEN
> It's coming out of Langely.

Carter can just barely contain his face from going totally white. Ryan as well starts to realize what's happening...

Carter bolts into another room, dialing his cell.

> CARTER
> Yea, get me Bannings!

EXT. SAFE HOUSE - DRIVEWAY - CONTINUOUS

Ryan pulls up in the car with the president. He helps him out.
The other bomb techs rush out, helping the president inside.

INT. SAFEHOUSE - CONTINUOUS

The bomb techs usher the president back to the area where they
have monitors and tools set up for disarmament.

> BOMB TECH #1
> We're at 28 minutes...

Suddenly, A BREAKING NEWS UPDATE FLASHES ON
THE TV SCREEN!

Carter paces on the phone, frantic.

> CARTER
> (frantic)
> You have to sequester the bank
> accounts.
> (hearing something he
> doesn't like)
> No, it's a trap! You have to slap them
> with a gag order!

> NEWS ANCHOR
> This just in: shocking new
> developments in the Al Fahad terrorist
> campaign on Pittsburgh, PA. Using
> the publicly available Swiss bank, now
> confirmed to belong to Mikel Razanov,
> hundreds of financial experts and
> investigative journalists have been able
> to piece together what has become a
> very troubling puzzle- one with

profound implications.

On TV though, the news anchor broaches the point:

> NEWS ANCHOR
> ...A number of news organization and
> financial institutions are coming to the
> same conclusion: The Al-Fahad
> terrorist network appears to be... a
> CREATION OF THE CIA.
>   (ALT: "...is in fact...a
> C.I.A. CREATION)

It's almost as if the nuke has actually detonated. The president looks up, the bomb techs look up... Ryan looks up...

All them... seeing the news...

The president's HEART RATE MONITOR STARTS TO BEEP WILDLY... The techs get back to working on the bomb.

And Carter... having expected this... sees that he is literally powerless to stop what's coming next.

> NEWS ANCHOR
> The money funding Mikel Razanov's
> terror campaign was initially deposited
> by an AVCO oil, a middle eastern
> company with offices in Pittsburgh,
> PA- this corporation is now believed to
> be a front for the Central Intelligence
> Agency to make fiscal transactions out
> of their international jurisdiction.

However, Ryan realizes something. He rushes over to a laptop, pulls up Razanov's account.

NEWS ANCHOR
US citizens are already assembling on
the streets in protest.

CARTER
(realizing)
That's why he sent the media his
account...

MONTAGE.

CHAOS.

- American citizens, assembling, protesting. SCREAMING IN
RAGE.

- On TELEVISION- newscasters, experts, all rage about the
CIA and leap to conclusions.

EXPERT
Who is to say we didn't pay for 9/11 to
happen?

- Carter, on his phone, growing even more frantic.

CARTER
I don't give a shit about their first
amendment rights! These guys are
gonna' burn the country down.

- ON THE NEWS- a SPOKESPERSON for the ACLU-

ACLU
This is really an attack on the liberties
of the American people and the
foundation of the United States of
America!

- Razanov, in his hideout, watching the news unfold. Prideful.

- Broadcasters reporting that the prisoners at Guantonomo bay are rioting, in light of the revelations, and demanding their release.

- The ACLU spokesperson demands that prisoners at Guantonomo Bay BE RELEASED.

INT. SAFE HOUSE - ROOM - SAME

THE NUKE TIMER: 17 Minutes...

The bomb techs, sweating, typing on their keyboards, feeding a fiber optic camera through the bomb... looking at the image on the video feed....

Bomb Tech #1, sweaty, grits at something.

> BOMB TECH #2
> What?

> BOMB TECH #1
> There's no bypass trigger.

He wipes his face.

> BOMB TECH #1
> We need another plan.

Ryan strikes the laptop keys, going through Razanov's account. Carter enters.

> CARTER
> What are you doing?

> RYAN
> I can still find this man.

CARTER
The account was a trap for us, Ryan-
the country's imploding!

MONTAGE

- More destruction- American citizens rioting at the assembling
police. News footage of riots, chaos. Flag burning.

- Newscaster:

NEWSCASTER
Clearly we have been funding terror
attacks against ourselves, all in the
name of suppressing the American
people! The war on terror is a FALSE
GOD!

- People marching on Washington. Mad as Hell. Demanding
the CIA be dismantled.

NEWSCASTER (V.O.)
The real terrorism is coming from our
protectors!

INT. SAFE HOUSE - CONTINUOUS

Ryan continues going through Razanov's account, Carter
hanging overhead.

RYAN
Look. The first withdrawal was in the
UK, London. Cash withdrawals at
Heathrow International, then nothing
until he gets to the US.

CARTER

Meaning?

Ryan grits his teeth, thinking...

Then it hits him. He flashes back to Art, the banker, telling him that the terrorists needed a point man.

> RYAN
> (realizing)
> He laundered the money.

He looks over at the banker's iPAD. He signals a TECH over.

> RYAN
> If someone did their banking on this,
> (re: the iPAD)
> Could you get into the account?

The tech sits down, plugs his laptop into the iPAD.

> TECH
> Whose is it?

> RYAN
> A banker's...

CONTINUE DESTRUCTION MONTAGE

- Things are really getting bad now. People rioting through stores. Breaking shit. All groups of people chanting, "BURN USA! BURN USA!"

- Razanov, strolling through his compound, so proud and arrogant. He espouses to his minions.

> RAZANOV
> Today, the world will witness the
> collapse of history's largest empire.

And it will be at the hands of its own
people!

- Media coverage of the riots at Guantonomo, the prisoners now
rushing the guards.

- A protestor screaming-

> PROTESTOR
> It is WE who are the enemy! We must
> pay! We must pay for our sins!

INT. SAFE HOUSE - CONTINUOUS

The tech pecks at his laptop- CLICKS ENTER- files cascade
over the iPAD's screen.

> TECH
> Bingo.

Ryan searches through.

> RYAN
> They used the banker's account to
> make all the purchases.

He looks through the account...

> RYAN
> April 2011, a transaction with First
> Industrial for 200 thousand dollars.

The tech clicks on it.

> CARTER
> You think that's where Razanov is?

> RYAN

I know that's where he is.

MONTAGE

- America, burning. A shot of the Capitol building. Flames eating the roof. Reportage of freedom militias rising, kidnapping congressmen, dragging them out on the steps of the Capitol building... and EXECUTING THEM IN COLD BLOOD.

EXT. SAFE HOUSE - SAME

Ryan heads out to the car, loading his gun. Carter chases after. Ryan TUNES a CB RADIO, clips it on his waist.

> RYAN
> Let's stay in contact. If I get anything,
> I'll be in touch.

> CARTER
> How is finding this guy going to stop
> what's happening?

> RYAN
> It won't.

> CARTER
> Then what are you doing?

> RYAN
> I don't want to spend the rest of my life
> on death row.

> CARTER
> He's a terrorist, Ryan!

> RYAN
> He's the only one with any credibility
> right now.

CARTER
And what if we can't disarm this bomb?

Ryan stops.

RYAN
Then you'll have to make the right
decision.

CARTER
We do that and they win.

RYAN
Do you think anyone will really care?

Carter, shocked by this. Ryan gets in the car, starts it up.

CARTER
(recovering)
The techs can't stop it, Ryan. There's
not enough time.

Ryan... stopping...

CARTER
But one of the engineers showed us a
tunnel out on the Parkway that could
contain the blast. We're already
evacuating the surrounding area.

RYAN
And why are you telling me this?

CARTER
Because they figured out there's a lag
on the heart monitor... as long as they
switch it within a few seconds, the

motherboard won't know the
difference.

(MAYBE INCLUDE A SHOT OF THE BOMB TECH
OBSERVING THE IV IN THE PRESIDENT'S
ARM...CONNECTED TO THE BOMB) YES!

Ryan glares in his eyes, understanding. Defiant...

> CARTER
> The bomb needs a heart, Ryan. At
> least until detonation.

> RYAN
> I'm sorry, agent Carter. But these
> people are not worth dying for.

Ryan squeals off, leaving Carter.

MONTAGE

- The chaos continues. Freedom fighters call into call-in shows,
screaming about how shitty the country is, how awful the CIA is,
and how they oughtta' DO something about it!

- News footage of the director of justice announcing that all
prisoners of the war on terror... will be released.

- Razanov, watching all of this...

> RAZANOV
> Be free my brothers.

- Ryan drives on the highway. Fast. Swerving in and out of
traffic. Determination in his eyes.

INT. SAFE HOUSE - CONTINUOS

Carter, somber, enters back in. Bomb tech one, readies a hand on the president's IV.

> BOMB TECH #1
> As soon as I remove it, we're only going to have a few seconds before the motherboard recognizes there's no heart rate.
> (to Carter)
> Are you sure about this?

He rolls up his sleeve, ready for the IV...

INT. RAZANOV'S HIDEOUT - SAME

Razanov sits before a videorecorder. Readies himself. One of his minions hits record. Nods.

> RAZANOV
> (staring into the lens)
> ...As I have been saying all along... I am not your enemy... I am merely... the messenger. I come to you to show you that your government wants only oppression for you. After today's events, your leaders will declare a state of martial law. They will fight back. An assault rifle in every soldier's hand. Barbed wire on every street corner. Camps will be open for those who resist. You will see that your country... your people... are not ready for freedom. So it is we... who are here to pick up the pieces.

EXT. INDUSTRIAL WAREHOUSE (RAZANOV'S

HIDEOUT) - SAME

F-18s fly overhead, toward the city. DISTANT
EXPLOSIONS. The sounds of World War III happening...

Ryan pulls up. On the radio, the announcer reads that
"GROUND TROOPS ARE BEING ASSEMBLED AND
ARE BEING DEPLOYED IN ALL URBAN AREAS..."

He gets out, moves to the back of his car, opens the tailgate. He
opens his bag-revealing the C-4 he took from the terrorist's SUV.

He readies it...

INT. SAFE HOUSE - SAME

The nuke timer clicks past 7 minutes...

The bomb tech pinches the IV stuck in the president's arm. The
tech takes a deep breath... looking at Carter, making sure he's
ready...

The president, sweating... looks in Carter's eyes... nodding.

>   PRESIDENT
>   (to Carter)
>   Thank you.

The bomb tech removes the IV from the president. The heart
monitor BEEPS! Failing. He sticks it into Carter's arm.

The heart monitor STABILIZES.

>   BOMB TECH #1
>   We're clear.

INT. RAZANOV'S HIDEOUT - RAZANOV'S ROOM -
SAME

Razanov finishes up giving his confession...

> RAZANOV
> You're country has been in dire need of
> a savior... and I am willing to make that
> sacrifice for you...

The terrorist hits "STOP" on the camera.

> TERRORIST
> Very good, sir. I will send it out.

The terrorist leaves. Razanov's CB BLEEPS.

> YAKOV (V.O.)
> Mikel.

> RAZANOV
> (answering it)
> Yes.

> YAKOV
> It is the American. He's here.

> RAZANOV
> Then kill him.

> YAKOV
> I can't.

Razanov, confused.

EXT. SAFE HOUSE - SAME

The bomb techs load the president in the back of their SUV,
shutting the door. They take off.

Carter, NOW CARRYING THE SUITCASE NUKE, hooked

up to it, hops in his SUV.

Arlen moves with him. Helps the case in.

> ARLEN
> The police have the tunnel closed off.
> You just have to make it to the middle.

Carter nods.

> ARLEN
> Carter.

Arlen sticks his hand out. The two men shake. Carter gets in, shuts the door. Takes off.

The timer clicking past 5 minutes...

INT. RAZANOV'S HIDEOUT - RAZANOV'S ROOM - SAME

The door opens... Yakov stepping in...

Razanov turns from the window...

Yakov doesn't look happy; he steps aside, revealing why...

Ryan enters... his <u>CHEST STRAPPED WITH BLOCKS OF C-4...</u> He holds his cell phone... clutching it as a suicide bomber might... finger on the "SEND" button.

> RYAN
> You thought I would just walk away...
> but I'm here. Now.

EXT. HIGHWAY - SAME

Carter's SUV screeches onto the highway.

INSIDE SUV

He drives. The nuke timer clicking down...

It hits 2 minutes...

He slams the gas.

INT. RAZANOV'S HIDEOUT - SAME

Razanov can only smile, seeing Ryan standing there... looking like a die-hard suicide bomber... cell phone out... C-4 clinging to his chest.

> RAZANOV
> (to his Yakov)
> Leave us.

Yakov leaves, shutting the door. Ryan stands there, holding the cell phone outward, making sure Razanov sees the C-4.

> RAZANOV
> This is to make me confess?

> RYAN
> To clear my name.

> RAZANOV
> It would mean taking your life...

> RYAN
> If it comes to that.

> RAZANOV
> But isn't that why you abandoned us...
> in favor of the CIA?

Ryan... surprised he knows...

                         RYAN
        I realized my cause over there wasn't
        worth it.

                       RAZANOV
        And what that was...?

                         RYAN
        To find Bin Laden. And kill him.

Razanov smiles...

                       RAZANOV
        After all this time... you were always
        just a gung-ho infidel.

INT. CARTER'S SUV - SAME

Carter drives... fast...

Past the windshield he sees the tunnel approaching. Car still
roam on the highway.

                        CARTER
                (triggering his radio)
        SOMEONE GET THESE PEOPLE
        OUT OF HERE!

He tosses the CB. Eyes the nuke...

...as it hits seconds now...

He drives the SUV into the tunnel... driving further in...

...the nuke timer dwindles... 8, 7, 6, 5...

He grips the steering wheel.

INT. RAZANOV'S HIDEOUT - SAME

Razanov, looking as if he has a wild card up his sleeve, still observing Ryan holding the C-4.

> RAZANOV
> Well, I must warn you to think twice about it then...

Razanov unravels an IV, sticks it in his arm...

> RAZANOV
> While death for your cause may come easy to you... actions do have consequences.

He plugs it into a large case...

> RAZANOV
> Whereas the president's death would stop detonation... mine would only ensure it.

He opens the case... to reveal the inner-workings of a SUITCASE NUKE, wired with C-4, centered by a digital timer.

INT. CARTER'S SUV - SAME

Carter, in the middle of the tunnel, hearing the timer... hit 0:00:00... he screams... SLAMMING THE BREAKS...

But nothing happens. Instead... HAIL TO THE CHIEF PLAYS on the IPAD ATTACHED TO THE BOMB, playing a video of a flag waving.

Carter... eyes still closed... peaks over...

The bomb... just sitting there.

A dud.

                    CARTER
                  (relieved)
            You son of a bitch.

INT. RAZANOV'S HIDEOUT - SAME

Razanov flicks on a heart monitor in his suitcase... it beeps to life... next to the words "ARMED."

Ryan's radio crackles. It's Carter.

                  CARTER (V.O.)
            Ryan! Ryan! It was a fake! I repeat,
            the nuke was a fake! We're in the clear!

Razanov flicks a switch on the nuke, the timer registers at 10 minutes... and counting. 9:59...9:58...9:57...Ryan's face goes pale.

Ryan... gulping... watching the nuke click away... realizing that the situation is becoming quickly fucked...

                    RYAN
            So you're willing to die... to guarantee
            your legacy.

Razanov smiles... the nuke continues to click away.

                  RAZANOV (V.O.)
            When I served under the hand of
            Osama Bin Laden... do you know what
            his greatest regret was? That he did not
            fly those planes in the towers on 9/11
            himself. That he stayed behind... to
            grow old... and fearful. He taught me...
            that if a soldier is not willing to sacrifice
            himself... then he must be sacrificed for

the greater good.

Ryan... realizing something.

> RYAN
> That's why you picked the Snyder
> building...

> RAZANOV
> I needed some way to cover up the
> transaction. After all... who would
> believe me... if they knew I'd sold out
> my master... for a fast 25 million dollars.

> RYAN
> You were the informant who gave us
> Bin Laden.

> RAZANOV
> And your C.I.A. paid me handsomely.

A beat. Razanov caulks his gun, smiling, indicating to Ryan it is time to die...

> RYAN
> That was the endgame.

Ryan tries to muster a smile... still holding up the cell phone... He lowers to his knees...

> RAZANOV
> To make your country turn on itself.

...looking up at Razanov...

> RYAN
> And the bomb...?

Razanoz aims the gun right at Ryan's head-

RAZANOV
Tying off loose ends I'm afraid.

BANG! But it's not Ryan who gets shot. Rather, it is Razanov.

Behind Ryan, at the open door... is YAKOV- a smoking gun in his hand.

Razanov can hardly contain his surprise, his gut bleeding out. He gazes at the fatal wound... dropping to his knees... then at Yakov... at the door, smoking gun in his hand...

YAKOV
You betrayed our master...

Yakov tosses over an iPAD... It's playing the news... the logo in the corner of the screen, the info crawl... but it's playing live footage of...

RAZANOV, dying...

It's as if the news is in the room with him, filming him at this moment...

Razanov doesn't understand, confused...

NEWS BROADCASTER (V.O.)
If you're just joining us now, we are
currently joined with the terrorist who
bombed the Snyder building, Ryan
Taylor, via a live video chat...

Razanov's eyes BULGE IN HORROR... as he looks up at Ryan... holding the cell phone. All along he thought it had been a trigger for the C-4... but it was only just recording his every word.

RAZANOV
No!

NEWS BROADCASTER (V.O.)
Startling revelations, ladies and
gentlemen. As it turns out, the 25
million paid to Mikel Razanov by the
CIA... was in fact a REWARD for the
terrorist mastermind giving us leading
to the capture of Osama Bin Laden...

Yakov looks at a dying Razanov with such hatred...

YAKOV
You betrayed us all...

Ryan still sits on his knees, still aiming the cell phone. His
expression flat.

And Yakov... a man disillusioned...

YAKOV
I believed in you... but you betrayed us
all...

And he just leaves the doorframe.

Leaving just Ryan there... to witness Razanov's last moments.

Ryan hits "END" on the cell phone. He rises over the fading
Razanov, who has fallen to his side... bleeding out.

The heart monitor attached to the nuke begins to BEEP... as the
life drains out of Razanov... the monitor beeps faster and faster...
closing in on detonation.

RAZANOV
But you only wanted your freedom...

Ryan closes the phone... moving over to Razanov...

> RAZANOV
> I could have given you... your freedom
> back.

Ryan pulls the IV line out of Razanov's arm... and slides it into his own arm... making the heart monitor stabilize...

> RYAN
> I don't negotiate with terrorists.

Razanov... his eyes reaching deep into Ryan's... the life fading... his last breath slipping away...

Razanov's eyes close...

And Ryan... alone now with the nuke...

The timer dwindling past 6 minutes...

He triggers his mic.

> RYAN
> Hey Carter.

> CARTER (V.O.)
> Yea, Ryan.

> RYAN
> Clear the tunnel.

Fade up the CLOSING MUSIC...

As Ryan leaves with the nuke...

EXT. HIGHWAY - LATER

The nuke, nestled in the front seat, the timer dwindling past 1 minute...

...the heart monitor stabilized.

Ryan... at the wheel... the setting sun striking him in the eyes...

...A vast tunnel full of blackness approaches...

...closer...

...The timer nearing zero...

...closer...

And Ryan... Fading daylight stabbing at his peaceful eyes...

...until the tunnel engulfs him in complete darkness.

"Forbid it, Almighty God! I know not what course others may take; But as for me, give me liberty... ...or give me death."
- Patrick Henry, March 23, 1775

THE END.

ABOUT THE AUTHOR

Tom Getty is an award winning writer, director, and actor, known for *Emulation* (2010), *Unbelief* (2003) and *American Writer* (2004). He attended the University of Pittsburgh and graduated Cum Laude with a degree in Communications. He began directing and writing when he was 8 years old.

www.ingramcontent.com/pod-product-compliance
Lightning Source LLC
Chambersburg PA
CBHW020038040426
42331CB00030B/16